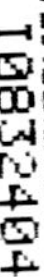
I0832404

BAPTIST CHURCH, CHAPEL, AND PARSONAGE, CANTON.

THE

Canton Baptist Memorial,

BEING A HISTORICAL DISCOURSE

DELIVERED BEFORE THE

Baptist Church in Canton, Mass.,

AT THE CELEBRATION OF THEIR

FIFTIETH ANNIVERSARY,

Wednesday, June 22, 1864,

BY THE PASTOR, REV. THERON BROWN.

Gather up the fragments that remain, that nothing be lost.—John vi. 12.

BOSTON:
PRESS OF GEO. C. RAND & AVERY, No. 3, CORNHILL.
1865.

INTRODUCTION.

The year 1864 was pre-eminently a year of jubilees. The American Tract Society, the Northern Baptist Education Society, and the American Baptist Missionary Union, completed their half-century then, and honored their birthdays with fit and imposing ceremonies; while Brown University among the colleges, and Fitchburg among the cities, called home glad assemblies of friends to the festivities of their first centennial. Of humbler corporations, remarkable for completing that year the magic fifty, besides our own, were the Baptist churches in Sharon, Westboro', and Webster. The Baptist Church in Warren, R.I., reached the end of its hundredth year on the 15th of November, 1864, and observed the day by a re-union and religious services.

It is perhaps unprecedented in the records of church anniversary solemnities that the occasion transpired without the attendance of a single former pastor. In the case of this church, which could count between twenty and thirty living ministers who had at some time, for a longer or shorter term, cast in their lot with her, and retained yet a tender interest in her life and welfare, to find not one old pastor, and but two of her former preachers, among her guests on the morning of her semi-centennial jubilee, was a grievous and seemingly needless disappointment. Even the first, or as good as the first, of the ministers of the church, the venerable patriarch of ninety, was alive that day in a distant State.

There was, however, but little room for blame in any quarter. The haste of the preparations and the imperfect acquaintance with post-office addresses rendered the disappointment in question almost if not quite unavoidable, and it must be written among the lost opportunities with as much content as may be.

The Jubilee Exercises.

The fiftieth anniversary of the Canton Baptist Church fell on Wednesday, the very week-day on which it was constituted. The weather was warm and bright; and the church, with many visiting friends, assembled in the Baptist meeting-house at ten o'clock, A.M., for religious services. The anthem, "Wake the Song of Jubilee," was sung by the choir, after which the sixth chapter of Ezra was read by the pastor, and prayer was offered by Father David Curtis of East Stoughton. The hymn, "I love thy kingdom, Lord," was then sung, and immediately followed by the Memorial Sermon. After the sermon, the anthem, "Daughter of Zion, awake from thy sadness," was sung; Rev. A. F. Mason of Meriden, Conn., offered prayer; and, after the singing of another anthem, the congregation was dismissed, to meet again in the afternoon.

At half-past one, P.M., the church and visitors re-assembled around a bountiful feast in the dining-hall of the Massapoag House. A blessing was invoked by Father Curtis; and, after a hearty discussion of the viands upon the table, letters were read from former pastors Moses Curtis, Henry Clark, T. C. Tingley, David B. Ford, and George W. Hervey, expressing their regrets that they were unable to be present. Short addresses were then made by Father Curtis, Rev. Joseph W.

Eaton, Rev. A. F. Mason, and Deacon Luther Hewins, containing interesting allusions to "the former days;" and Messrs. Addison Boyden and Roland F. Alger, of South Dedham, did ample justice, in stirring and pithy speeches, to the progress and claims of the Baptist cause in New England. Remarks were made also by the pastor; and, after singing "Coronation" together, the jubilee assembly broke up. Rev. J. W. Olmsted, D.D., of the "Watchman and Reflector," arrived too late for the festivities, but made one of a party in an excursion to the old Blackman House to see the room where, fifty years before, the thirty-five constituent members of the church signed their names to the Covenant and Articles of Faith. In the evening, an interesting meeting was held in the chapel; where former preachers took part in the services, and closed with worship a happy and memorable day.

In the following history, wherever I have occasion to refer the reader to the church-records, I have inserted in the text parentheses ( ) containing the figures of the page.

Proper names introduced in capitals are those of pastors or evangelists of the church.

Tables of statistics and other important particulars respecting the church, which would have embarrassed the pages of the Memorial, I have placed in the Appendix.

I have to express my obligations to members of the church, past and present, resident and non-resident; to the former pastors and ministers; to many intelligent friends in the town, not connected with us; and to the Editors of the "Watchman and Reflector," and the "Christian Secretary," for their valuable aid in furthering my inquiries and collecting desired information. Special acknowledgments are due to Rev. Kendall Brooks, Rev. J. Ricker, Rev. William Hurlin, Rev. David

Benedict, D.D.; Rev. Baron Stow, D.D.; Rev. Cornelius A. Thomas, D.D.; Professors Ripley, Hovey, and Train, of Newton; Mr. James M. Whitehead, Assistant Treas. Bap. Home Miss. Soc.; Mr. Albert Mason, Mr. Jonas Evans, Ellis Ames, Esq., Alfred E. Giles, Esq., Mrs. Hannah W. Ober, Mrs. Martha H. Moore, Mrs. Abigail Maynard, Mrs. Nabby Capen, Miss S. L. Kimball, and Bro. Alonzo Bunker, Assistant Librarian in Newton Theological Seminary, for their kind assistance in searching for and communicating facts, and for papers lent to me by them, which have enabled me to certify many doubtful points in the history.

I should say here, that, though the body of this history is styled a "Memorial Sermon," the sermon, as originally delivered, forms but the nucleus of the book. Facts and corrections accumulated; and, as what was worth doing at all was worth doing well, the sermon grew into a volume.

THERON BROWN.

Canton, June, 1865.

THE CANTON BAPTIST MEMORIAL.

A Historical Discourse.

MEMORIAL SERMON.

"Then Darius the king made a decree, and search was made in the house of the rolls where the treasures were laid up in Babylon. And there was found at Achmetha, in the palace that is in the province of the Medes, a roll; and therein was a record thus written: In the first year of Cyrus the king, the same Cyrus the king made a decree concerning the house of God at Jerusalem, Let the house be builded, the place where they offered sacrifices, and let the foundations thereof be strongly laid; the height thereof threescore cubits, and the breadth thereof threescore cubits, with three rows of great stones, and a row of new timber; and let the expenses be given out of the king's house."—EZRA vi. 1–4.

ON many accounts it is an excellent thing to look over the records of former years. Exhortations and precepts become forceless after a while if they are not alternated with examples. Simon Peter knew this; and his sermon in the second chapter of Acts would have shown, if he had never said it in so many words elsewhere, that he calculated on the best effects when he stirred up the minds of his hearers "*by way of remembrance.*" After setting a good example himself in many things, and pointing out the good examples of the prophets, and the perfect example of Jesus to his followers, it was right and thoughtful in him to put down some of that same kind of admonition on parchment, saying, as he did so, "*I will endeavor that ye may be able after my decease to have these things always in remembrance.*" So did Paul know it; and he never said a thing more certain to stimulate the drooping courage of his Hebrew brethren than when he bade them "*call to remembrance the former days.*"

If it had not been for the example of Cyrus, recorded in that old roll, Darius would never have stirred himself to help the Jews, and they never would have built their temple, and the church would still have sat by the rivers of Babylon. But the old records were found, and carefully looked over; and there God's people read what made their hearts gladder than they had been for years, — a standing order for re-organizing their ancient worship, with particulars of the work, and a statement of all the facilities; and the effect was, that they said one to another, immediately, "Come, let us go up! Here is the royal sanction given to our fathers, and it is just as good for us. Let us stir ourselves and build and prosper!" Then down fell the timber in the king's forest, and forth rolled the great blocks and slabs out of the king's quarries, and up went the walls. Woe to the man that should hinder them!

We have thought it good, dear brethren, to look over the records of *our* past to-day, to find where *our* fathers started with the royal sanction; what trials they suffered, and how well they bore them; how jealously they watched God's heritage; how well they wrought, and how warmly they prayed; what enemies they had, and what sins; their worship, their discipline, their charity, their hopes, and their fears. May the review stimulate us to new hope and heartiness in building up Zion! May it exercise our sympathies healthfully, and divert us from our own little ills and discouragements by reviving in us the sense of fellowship in nobler struggles, and the love of a common cause!

Fifty years ago, the red scourge of war which we feel to-day afflicted the fathers who cultivated the fields around us. Then, as now, the sweat of the face, by which man eats his bread, was wrung out by burdensome taxes, which fastened upon his estate as well as upon the comforts and luxuries that stocked it; and the families of our ancestors were as familiar as we with the weekly news of desolation and blood. Then, as now, the whole face of society wore the frown of "hard times;" and "the cry of the poverty that distressed alike the people and the priest resounded from every hill and every valley."* Both England and Algiers had drawn the sword against this country; and during the year in which this

* Fast Day Sermon of Rev. William Ritchie.

In this place, it is interesting to note the curious proof of national progress during the last fifty years, furnished in the contrast of the old and new military equipments, quotas, and bounties. In April 4, 1812, the ammunition stock of the town was looked to by a special committee, which reported "six quarter-casks of powder (one hundred and fifty pounds), one hundred and twelve and one-half pounds of balls, four hundred flints, and six camp-kettles," all carefully held in charge by Elijah Dunbar, Esq. The quota of Massachusetts (then including the District of Maine) was a hundred thousand men; and Canton volunteers were offered fourteen dollars a month, and two dollars bounty. — *Town Records, vol. i, pp.* 245, 253.

church commenced its existence, no immediate prospect appeared that the strife would cease. The people of that day were not a whit behind us in fellowship with toil and trouble. Neither in their civil nor religious privileges were they a whit better off than we. The hardship of war was aggravated to the New-England fathers of that generation by their honest belief that it was unnecessary and unwise. Nor was their President, in any quality that makes the honest, fearless statesman, at all to be compared to ours; while, ecclesiastically, their good consciences suffered under the tyranny of the "half-way covenant," and the new theology which was its offspring, and which had gradually made its way, in spite of "the ponderous logic of Jonathan Edwards, the burning rhetoric of Edward Griffin, and the withering sarcasm of Lyman Beecher," to a power and influence that well-nigh swallowed up Harvard College, and palsied half the heart of Calvinistic New England before it was aware.

In a struggle where all evangelical faith was interested for life or death, it was no time for the Baptists to be at ease in Zion. The voice of Stillman* had hardly ceased to echo from the old meeting-house by the "Mill-pond;" and the trumpet tones of Baldwin were heard with no uncertain sound, rallying the followers of Jesus round the prayer-meeting and the baptismal covenant; and, nearer home, the humbler but no less faithful witness of Elder Joel Briggs,† of Randolph, admonished the ungodly of "righteousness, temperance, and a judgment to come." For more than sixty years, this neighborhood had known no revival of religion. The half-way covenant, in force since 1657, with its consequent curse of an unconverted church membership, and the long habit of depending on *compulsory taxation* for the support of the ordinances of the gospel, contributed largely to produce a spiritual coldness that rendered the case of professed Christians apparently as desperate as that of the most notorious unbelievers.

The only church in Canton was the church of the standing order, now Unitarian, at the Corner, then under the pastoral

* Died March, 1807.

† A grand-daughter of this old-time preacher (Mrs. J. Wiswall) is now a member of this church.

care of Rev. William Ritchie. Founded in 1717, this church had learned to regard itself indisputably entitled to the ecclesiastical control of the whole "North Precinct;"* and as early as the days when Whitefield, in his first itinerations through New England, electrified the people of Dorchester, it had set itself, pastor and people, resolutely against him, and closed the pulpit in "South Village"† so effectually to his offered entrance, that it is said he foretold in prophetic indignation the spiritual barrenness of their future years. Be that as it may, an influence more potent than any words of Whitefield, whether to curse or bless, now began to stir in the community, and awaken signs of religious life.

In the fall of 1811, Elder Briggs held by request a meeting in a school-house, about five miles from this spot, in the east part of the town, now known as York Street. The Spirit of God had prepared the way; and one, already in the joy of a good hope through grace, was able at that meeting to testify for Christ.‡ Others, who had been secretly serious, went away deeply affected by the sermon; and the impressions of the evening were such, that the good Elder felt justified in making another appointment. He continued the meetings here with most cheering results. His preaching began to be thronged by curious and then by willing listeners. It was the voice of Ezekiel prophesying to the dry bones. Opposition awoke with the revival of religious feeling, and kept pace with the success of gospel truth. Part of it came from that denominational prejudice, which, from the beginning of a divided Christianity, has never been able to look comfortably on the severe simplicity of New Testament Protestantism; and part of it came from the natural malice of wickedness, which habitually sets itself against pure religion. Mr. Ritchie saw no good in the new movement that was making such inroads on his parish. He commenced a series of afternoon § lectures, in private dwellings, among his

* Embracing Canton, Stoughton, and Sharon.

† Canton was Dorchester South Village, prior to 1726; afterwards, Stoughton, North Precinct.

‡ Supposed to be Sister Caty Tucker.

§ The fact that the Baptists held their meetings in the evening was used against

people, to counteract it. He sent for Mr. Whittaker of Sharon * to denounce it; and some of the invectives of that preacher against the Baptists are remembered to this day as specimens of that bitterness which was then everywhere felt towards the despised sect. The good Canton parson even made appointments himself at the York school-house, and strove, by partially modelling his own meetings after those of Elder Briggs, to satisfy, while he rebuked the spiritual agitation which was bearing so many away to the "fanaticism" of the Baptists. "They went out from us," he quoted in one of his sermons, "because they were not of us;" and he spoke the truth.

Boys and girls caught the tone of popular raillery, and repeated at school, to the children of their newly awakened neighbors, the sarcasms of their parents on the "Dippers" and "New Lights." The ridiculed sect accepted the nicknames, and gloried in them. A quaint old hymn, much sung by them in their meetings during those unpopular days, shows in what estimation they held their opprobrious titles.

"Come, all who are new lights indeed,
Who are from sin and bondage freed:
From Egypt's land we took our flight;
For God has given us a new light.

Long time we with the wicked trod,
And madly ran the sinful road;
Against the gospel we did fight,
Scared at the name of a New light.

At length the Lord in mercy called,
And gave us strength to give up all:
He gave us strength to choose aright
A portion with despised New lights.

Despised by man, upheld by God,
We're marching on the heavenly road:
Loud hallelujahs we will sing
To Jesus Christ, the New lights' King," &c.

This hymn the little company of Baptist worshippers had

them; Mr. Ritchie choosing for his text, on one occasion, "They love darkness rather than light, because their deeds are evil."

* Minister of Sharon from 1799 to 1816. — *Hist. Coll. Mass.*

all by heart; and the low, sweet minor tune to which they sung it was well adapted to content the believers, and even impress and win opposers.

Meanwhile the ungodly community looked on and sneered, until, perchance, the secret influence would reach their own circle, and call one of their number away, when they would cling to him with the grasp of desperation, and exhaust all the resources of menace and ridicule to retain him in the service of Satan.

One man, who afterwards became a chief supporter in the despised denomination, and left his praise in the church and among his fellow-townsmen, was then a centre of attraction in this thoughtless company, and with his stories and his violin often gave life to the convivial group that gathered at his store. A lady about his own age, Mrs. Caty Tucker, who also became subsequently a member of this church, was instrumental in turning his attention first to the things of religion.

He attended the York School-house Meetings, secretly at first; but soon, constrained by the narrow watchfulness of his wild comrades, who missed him from his store, he put on more boldness; and God gave him grace to withstand their artillery of scorn. To show the estimate which the men of the world put upon the religious movement of that day, he himself stated with tears, when he related his religious experience, that before his conversion he verily thought he should be doing God service, and conveying a public benefit, to complain to the selectmen of the town, and have these revival-meetings abated as a common nuisance.

The work still went on. After Elder Briggs came other good ministers to the neighborhood, and preached through the ensuing spring. Week after week, in the school-houses and in the homes of the people, Allen of Mansfield, Nelson of Middleboro', Grafton of Newton, Gammell of Medfield, and Williams and Paul of Boston, and others besides them, less well remembered, stood up and proclaimed to the ungodly the unsearchable riches of Christ.

Elder Thomas Paul was a son of thunder. He was a colored man, pastor of the African Baptist (now Joy Street) Church,

Boston, and went by the name of "Black Paul." Wherever he preached, the place was too strait to hold the hearers; and his power over the feelings, solemnizing the most careless, and thrilling the most cold, is remembered by the few who live to regret that he could not have visited the place oftener than he did. "His understanding was vigorous, his imagination was vivid, his personal appearance was interesting, and his elocution was graceful." * The key and intonations of his voice in prayer are said to have strikingly resembled Dr. Baldwin's. He died April 14, 1831, with the very words of his great namesake upon his lips, "I am now ready to be offered, and the time of my departure is at hand. I have fought a good fight. I have finished my course. I have kept the faith: henceforth there is laid up for me a crown of righteousness which the Lord, the righteous Judge, shall give me at that day."

Elder Paul had a son who graduated with honors at Dartmouth College, a young man of fine talents, and much respected.

Williams was Elder ELISHA SCOTT WILLIAMS, formerly of Beverly. He belonged to the Baldwin-place Church, Boston, and intinerated among the feeble churches in surrounding towns. To him belongs the credit (as far as to any one man) of organizing this church.

On the 14th of April, 1812, occurred the first baptism in the town. It was Monday, and the four candidates, with their friends, stood by the Reservoir Pond in front of Mr. Ezra Tilden's, where the novelty of the occasion had drawn together a numerous throng, and one by one received immersion at the hands of Elder Joel Briggs. These four pioneers were Ezra Tilden, his wife Bethiah, his brother Abner Tilden, and Enos Upham. The impression produced by this baptismal scene, the first of its kind which most of the spectators had ever witnessed, was conciliatory and wholesome. The ancient record of the transaction quotes, in closing, the familiar line of Goldsmith, —

"Fools who came to scoff remained to pray."

Another transaction of a very different sort took place

* Baptist Magazine, vol. xv. p. 221.

shortly after, a record of which in this place will be essential to the completeness of the history. One or two parishioners of Mr. Ritchie had taken offence at some remarks of his in the pulpit on Good Friday, concerning the state of the country, and induced others to join them in a compact to evade the *ministerial tax.* It was understood then, that, if any citizen should regularly join a religious society differing from the standing order, he should be exempted from contributing to the support of the town minister; and these disaffected individuals, taking advantage of the late movement of the Baptists, determined to secure their co-operation, and form themselves into a new organization under the name of the "Baptist Society." The matter passed under consultation a few weeks; and at length, on the 27th of April, the following individuals subscribed their names, and reported themselves to the town as a separate society: —

Samuel Blackman,	Abner Tilden,	Nathaniel Billings, Jr.,
Nathan Tucker,	Benjamin Lewis,	Jesse Wentworth,
Samuel Tucker, Jr.,	Jabez Cobb,	Jabez Billings,
Ezra Tilden,	Samuel Canterbury,	Thaddeus Churchill,
Nathan Kinney,	Elijah Jordan,	Seth Wentworth,
Benjamin Gill, Jr.,	Elijah Hawes,	Oliver Wentworth,
Enos Upham,	Spencer Wentworth,	Isaac Mann.

The last was a member of the First Baptist Church in Randolph (now East Stoughton).*

It will be observed that seven of the twenty-one were persons who afterwards entered the communion of this church by baptism or experience. The society, however, never had any thing to do with the measures and work of the church. Indeed the two had no vital connection; and the formation of the "Baptist Society" claims a mention here only as an interesting antecedent event to the proper history of the Church.

Thus two influences, distant both in cause and design, — the Spirit of God and the spirit of democratic independency, — were simultaneously working to one good result.

Through the summer and fall, the small but growing company

* Canton Town Records, vol. i. pp. 229, 248–9. Tax-payers, joining the Baptist and other churches differing from the standing order, were obliged, until 1833, to give a certificate of their membership to the town-clerk, or they were still held liable to the ministerial tax.

E Lincoln.

of "New-Light" believers enjoyed a frequent repetition of baptismal seasons, the ordinance being administered sometimes by one and sometimes by another of the neighboring ministers, at the Ponkapog and Reservoir Ponds, and at Houghton's Pond in Milton, until a goodly number had united with the church in Randolph, and others stood in readiness to erect the standard of the cause upon the soil of Canton. During the year 1813, Mr. Ensign Lincoln of Boston, father of Mr. Joshua Lincoln, of the present firm of Gould & Lincoln, preached once a month in the old north school-house, now the little brown

dwelling-house that stands beside the new school-house at Ponkapog.

Ensign Lincoln was born in Hingham, Mass., Jan. 8, 1779, and bred to the trade of a printer. At the age of nineteen, he was converted under the preaching of Dr. Baldwin, and baptized by that good man into the fellowship of his church. He commenced business in Boston as a publisher in 1800, and was licensed to preach in 1811, but followed his secular calling till his death, Dec. 2, 1832. He was successful in business, an able and faithful evangelist, and a zealous Christian. For many years both before and after the building of the first meeting-house, he came frequently to Canton to preach on the Sabbath. His son Joshua relates that he used sometimes to drive the horse on those itinerations, while his father studied his sermons by the way. Mr. Lincoln's first issue as a publisher was an edition of Cowper's works, the first in this country.*

Before the close of this year, the little assembly of believers in Canton was re-enforced by several conversions in the south of Milton, where the work of the Holy Spirit had been felt; and, during the spring of 1814, the desire to form a Baptist Church eventuated in a resolution to call a council for this purpose.

In the house of Brother Ezra Tilden (the old one), then standing near the north-east shore of Reservoir Pond, was planted the germ of the Canton Baptist Church. Through various fortunes, God, we believe, has since owned it as an offshoot of the True Vine. There in the square front room, on the afternoon of the 29th of May, 1814, a goodly number of brethren and sisters of the same mind met to ask counsel of God, and advise with one another for their immediate embodiment into a church. Elder Elisha Williams of Boston was present, and acted as moderator and general adviser. It was voted to call a council on the 22d of the following month; and brethren Nathan Tucker, Ezra Tilden, and Friend Crane, were chosen a committee to invite the churches.

On Wednesday, the 22d of June, at eleven o'clock, A.M., precisely fifty years ago this hour, the pastors and delegates, or elders and messengers as they were then called, assembled, pursuant to invitation, in the east room of the house of Mr.

Samuel Blackman (still standing, and inhabited by his son

* Cyclopædia of Religious Knowledge, art. "E. Lincoln."

Winthrop) to assist in organizing the new church and to extend to it the right hand of ecclesiastical and Christian fellowship.

The following composed the council: —

Elder Elisha Williams, who was chosen Moderator; Elder Thomas Baldwin, of the Second Baptist (now Baldwin Place) Church in Boston, with delegates J. C. Ransford, Jacob Hilar, and Thomas Badger; Elder Joel Briggs, from the First Randolph (now East Stoughton) Baptist Church, with delegates Benjamin Mann and Jonathan Wales; Elder Daniel Sharp, from the Third Baptist (now Charles St.) Church, Boston, with delegates Thomas Kendall and Ensign Lincoln, who was chosen clerk; Elder William Gammell, from the Medfield Baptist Church, with delegates Benjamin Colburn and Abijah Fisher; and from the Baptist Church in Newton, Elder Joseph Grafton, with brethren Noah King, Elijah Corey, and Caleb Hobart. Elder Henry Kendall, of Maine, was also present. After the letters of the candidates who had previously been in church-fellowship * had been read, and the experiences of all had been related, the council heard and approved the Articles of Faith, and voted to adopt the thirty-five brethren and sisters, whose names were appended to it, into the fraternity of Baptist churches; whereupon a programme of exercises for the afternoon was immediately agreed upon, and the meeting adjourned.

After dinner, — and at that dinner the "fatted calf" was served: that first entertainment of the Canton Baptist Church at the house of Mr. Blackman, for many years well known as a Baptist tavern, has been surpassed in generous good cheer by few if any of its later commemorative banquets, or feasts of tabernacles, during the last fifty years,† — after dinner, the Church and Council removed to a pine-grove on the east side of the present Boston Road, a furlong or more south of Mr. Blackman's house, and about a hundred and

* At Randolph.

† Survivors of that day who assisted in serving the tables on that occasion agree in testifying that the guests (about three hundred in number) had before them, in course, two calves, the hams of two hogs, a bushel of shelled green peas, and between thirty and forty mince and custard pies, with the (then no less essential) accompaniment of a barrel of "old October."

twenty rods north-east from the Unitarian meeting-house. A large auditory had already assembled, and at about two o'clock the religious services were opened with prayer by Elder Joseph Grafton. After singing, Elder Thomas Baldwin preached the sermon from the First Epistle of John, fourth chapter, and seventh verse. "Beloved, let us love one another; for love is of God; and every one that loveth is born of God, and knoweth God." The theme could not have been more happily chosen, nor could any have treated it with greater ability and effect than the preacher.

Those who knew Dr. Baldwin, and loved him for his genial ways in social intercourse,* speak no less of his subduing power in the pulpit. On the rude platform in Spurr's Grove, those who remember tell us how his earnestness and pathos that day, as he urged upon his hearers the example and precept of the beloved disciple, moved their hearts, and impressed them into silent attention. After the sermon, Dr. Sharp presented the fellowship of the churches, Brother Oliver Houghton, the oldest member in the newly adopted flock, standing up to receive the right hand; and Elder William Gammell closed the services with prayer. A note of the occasion made soon after by the church-clerk says, "The assembly was large, the day pleasant, and the season joyfull"

The fine trees of the old grove have been cut down for timber; and the spot where those holy men stood and spoke their hearty God-speed to our infant church is grown up to shrub-oaks and brambles: but *they*, the sturdy fathers whose delight

* In private, Dr. Baldwin was not wanting in pleasant tales and sprightly sallies. On his arrival at the grove, while he was seeking for a good place to deposit his hat, he looked overhead, into the trees, and remarked to Elder Gammell, "I hope there are no monkeys up there," alluding to the then familiar school-book story of the traveller with the twelve red caps, eleven of which were stolen by monkeys while he was asleep in a forest. The good man's sociability did not waste itself, however, in mere pleasantries. He was full of anecdotes that had a moral to them. One aged lady, whose recollections of that day are quite vivid, tells us that he related the following incident at the house: It was in February (he said), 1805, at Sedgewick Me., when Elder Daniel Merrill with his wife and sixty-five members of his church, turned Baptists; and he was baptizing the candidates, assisted by Elder Elisha Williams. As one of the candidates was going down into the water, his faithful dog waded in behind him. "You may think the movement would provoke a laugh," said Elder Baldwin; "but it made an impression on me of a very different sort. I wished" — and his voice faltered with emotion — "that I could be as ready to follow my Master always as that dog was to follow his."

was in the law of the Lord, now sit under the shadow of the Tree of Life, that shall never be hewn down.

In the evening, an interesting service was held at the house of Mr. Blackman,* when Elder Gammell preached to the newly constituted church with old-fashioned aptness from Canticles iv. 16: "Awake, O north wind, and come, thou south; blow upon my garden, that the spices thereof may flow out. Let my Beloved come into his garden and eat his pleasant fruits." In the years that followed, that summons did not wholly lack its answer.

The Articles of Faith and Order subscribed to in the morning of that day by fourteen brethren and twenty-one sisters are as follows, with preamble and covenant: —

AS we have been baptized in the name of the Father, and of the Son, and of the Holy Ghost, upon a profession of our faith, and are desirous of being embodied into a church of our Lord Jesus Christ; so we do now make a declaration of the doctrines and practice which we believe, and promise to maintain.

FIRST.

We believe that the Scriptures of the Old and New Testaments are the word of God and the only rule of faith and practice.

SECOND.

That they contain and reveal the doctrine of the adorable Trinity in one God.

THIRD.

That they reveal the doctrine of particular election and redemption.

FOURTH.

That Adam was created in the image of God, holy, innocent, and happy.

FIFTH.

That all mankind are affected by his apostasy; are depraved, and in a ruined condition, from which there is no deliverance but by Jesus Christ.

* Mr. Blackman made himself memorable in the early history of the Baptists in Canton, not only by his unvarying hospitality to all who were identified with the cause, but by his habit of serving Baptist ministers gratis in the line of his trade. He was a blacksmith, and for many years shod the horses of all the Baptist preachers who came into the town, without charge. He was even known to *sharpen the ploughshares* of Baptist clerical farmers from neighboring towns, and bid them welcome to the work.

SIXTH.

That Jesus Christ was constituted from everlasting as the Covenant Head and Surety of his people.

SEVENTH.

That regeneration and sanctification are wrought in the soul by divine and efficacious grace.

EIGHTH.

That our justification in the sight of God is, by the imputed righteousness of Jesus Christ, received by faith alone.

NINTH.

That all who have been born again, and are real saints, will persevere in grace to glory.

TENTH.

That there will be a resurrection of the dead, both of the righteous and the wicked, who shall be rewarded according to their works; and the sentence then passed will be eternal.

ELEVENTH.

That Baptism and the Lord's Supper are standing ordinances of the gospel; and that none have a right to the Lord's table but professing and baptized believers.

Besides the belief of these doctrines, we likewise promise, as God shall enable us, to walk in the duties of this Covenant by which as a church we unite: that is to say, we will endeavor to order our conversation in the church and in the world as becometh the gospel of Christ; that we esteem it our duty to walk together in Christian affection with humility and watchfulness; that we will not forsake the assembling of ourselves together; we will watch over and admonish our brethren in love as the case and duty may require; we will not neglect the duty of prayer for ourselves and for all Christians, and for all mankind; we will sympathize with our brethren in their affliction and distress.

In the presence of God, angels, and this assembly, we do now assent to these doctrines and to this Covenant.

In witness whereof, we hereunto set our hands this twenty-second day of June, in the year of our Lord one thousand eight hundred and fourteen.*

Nathan Tucker.	Ezra Tilden, Jr.
Friend Crane.	Oliver Houghton.
Jason Houghton.	Benjamin Gill, 2d.
Lemuel Fuller, Jr.	Elijah Hawes.
Andrew Fadden.	Wales Withington.
Abner Tilden.	Enos Upham.
Nathaniel Tucker Davis.	Samuel Tucker, Jr.

* See Appendix, p. 1.

Names of Members: their Family Connection.

JANE WENTWORTH.	ABIGAIL GILL.
HANNAH TUCKER.	BATHSHEBA FULLER.
CATY TUCKER.	BETHIAH TILDEN.
ABIGAIL HILL.	MARY MORSE.
ABIGAIL BIRD.	REBECCA CRANE.
RUTH M'KENDRY.	CATY HOUGHTON.
RUTH HOUGHTON.	LUCINDA GILL.
LUCY ALLEN.	MARY HOUGHTON.
MILLA TUCKER.	OLIVE TUCKER.
ELIPHAL WHEELER.	ELIZA TUCKER.

RUTH BUSS.

To sketch the individual history of these first members of the Canton Baptist Church would take us beyond the limits of our present design. But it will not be out of place to identify the families to which they belonged. NATHAN TUCKER was the father of Brethren Nathan and Isaac Tucker, now members of the Harvard-street Church, Boston, and Rev. George Tucker of Maine. His only surviving daughter, the widow of the late Rev. Bradley Miner of Providence, now resides here, a member of this church. HANNAH TUCKER was the wife of Nathan Tucker. She still survives, and is here to-day, in her eighty-sixth year, to commemorate the fiftieth anniversary of the church which she aided in establishing. EZRA TILDEN was the father of Mrs. Andrew Lopez and Mrs. John Fisher, both now sisters in the Church. BETHIAH TILDEN was the wife of Ezra Tilden. FRIEND CRANE was the father of Mrs. Jephthah Crane, and the grandfather of Mrs. George Ames, both members of the church. His great grandson is here to-day, six years old, a son of Mrs. Ames.

REBECCA CRANE was the wife of Friend Crane.

OLIVER HOUGHTON had no children. MARY HOUGHTON was his wife; and JASON HOUGHTON was his cousin, and the father of Messrs. George and Charles Houghton, formerly members with us, but now resident in the State of New York. Another son was Mr. Ralph Houghton, who died long since, and whose daughter, Mrs. Elias Tucker, resides here, and is a member of the church. CATY HOUGHTON was the wife of Jason. The Houghtons all lived in Milton.

BENJAMIN GILL still survives, at the age of seventy-five,

and is here to-day in comfortable health, though unable to hear much that I say.

LEMUEL FULLER was the father of Mr. Daniel Fuller of this town, and grandfather of Rev. Oliver S. Fuller of Centreville, R.I., once a member of this church. BATHSHEBA FULLER was the wife of Lemuel. ELIJAH HAWES has connections residing at Tucker Hill. One of them, Alpheus Hawes, is his nephew. Bro. Hawes removed to Ohio, where it is supposed he still survives, as he was living at last accounts, and in good health. ANDREW FADDEN was a cousin of Mr. Nathaniel Wentworth of this town, a son of his father's sister. WALES WITHINGTON was a cousin of Brother Enos Withington of this church. He removed to Maine. His daughter, Mrs. Edmund Low, lives in town; he has also a son in Stoughton. ABNER TILDEN resided in South Street, or the old "Indian Lane."* He was the father of Sisters Julia and Mary Tilden,† and Sister Hiram Johnson, all members of this church. His widow, Mrs. Catharine Tilden, is also a member of the church: she is now residing on his homestead. ENOS UPHAM, brother to Mrs. Friend Crane, was the father of Mr. Abner Upham of this town. His five daughters, Rebecca, Sarah, Mary, Lorra Ann, and Clara, were all members of this church till death or removal from the village severed the fellowship of all but the last. NATHANIEL TUCKER DAVIS belonged in Milton. He removed to Hingham in 1827, and none of his relatives are found in this vicinity. SAMUEL TUCKER was the father of Messrs. Elias, Gerry, and Aaron Tucker of this town, the last a member of the church. Mrs. Ellis Ames and Sister Eunice Tucker are his daughters. CATY TUCKER was the wife of Samuel Tucker, and survived him until the 29th of April, 1863. JANE WENTWORTH was the mother of Mr. Seth Wentworth at "the Farms." ABIGAIL GILL was the mother of Bethiah Tilden, Ezra Tilden's wife. ABIGAIL HILL was a servant-girl. Her connections belonged elsewhere, and none of them are found in this vicinity. MARY MORSE has no

* So called from the Ponkapog Indians. In that street still lives Daniel Croud, a member of this church, and still a stalwart man at seventy-three, who carries in his veins the last blood of that ancient tribe.

† Now Mary Kimball.

relatives here: she married a Pike, and removed to Athol in 1831. ABIGAIL BIRD belonged in Stoughton, where her surviving relatives still reside. RUTH M'KENDRY was sister to Mrs. Caty Tucker, and also to Messrs. William and John M'Kendry, and Mrs. Clifford Belcher, sen., all now living in Canton; the last a member of the church. RUTH HOUGHTON* was the daughter of Jason Houghton. LUCINDA GILL was a sister of Benjamin Gill, and subsequently became the wife of Francis Mason, now Dr. Mason, of Toungoo, Burmah. LUCY ALLEN was an old lady at the time of the constitution of the church, and died May 12, 1816, being the first of the constituent members who departed this life in the communion, as Sister Caty Tucker, it is believed, was the latest. The relatives of Lucy Allen are found in the Tucker families who live at "the Farms." MILLA TUCKER lived in York Street. She went by the name of "Aunt Milly," and was ever a true friend to the cause to which she here subscribed, though obliged for certain reasons to serve the church by stealth. Contributions from Canton to Baptist Missions, and other interests connected with the denomination, appear on record from the very birth of the church, credited to "A Friend;" and it is said by those acquainted with the facts, that these anonymous charities were hers. Isaac Fenno, and Mrs. Vernon Messenger, of Boston; and Miss Ellen French, of the Dudley-street Baptist Church, Roxbury, — are grandchildren of "Aunt Milly."

OLIVE TUCKER was a sister of Samuel Tucker.

ELIPHAL WHEELER was the daughter-in-law of Mr. Samuel Wheeler who many years ago made a liberal donation to the church (Unitarian) at Canton Corner. The Tuckers at "the Farms" are her connections. ELIZA TUCKER was Mrs. Wheeler's sister. She died single, July 29, 1834, leaving her property to the Baptist cause.† RUTH BUSS, written afterwards in the records as *Sally* Buss, was sister to Mr. Peter Crane,

* Since Mrs. Ruth Clapp. She is still living with her husband in Franklindale, N.Y., aged about 75, and this summer (1865), made a visit with him to her friends in this neighborhood.

† "Like a good steward, what the Lord gave her she left in the bosom of the Church, $1,200." — *Epitaph on her Tombstone.*

the maternal grandfather of the celebrated Margaret Fuller, and of Chaplain Fuller,* of Waltham, who fell on the Rapidan.

This little company, now united under one covenant,† began more or less regularly to observe the Christian ordinances, holding their meetings mostly in the school-house at Blue Hill.(18) Their Sabbath supplies were various, the settlement of a pastor being, of course, out of the question at that early day, when the church, like its Master, had not where to lay its head; but Elder HENRY KENDALL was of all the preachers the best beloved, and to this day is of all the most vividly remembered by the few surviving members who were then in active service. He came to Canton a stranger at the time of the constitution of the church, having first been providentially led to this part of the country through his appointment as a member of the General Court from the District of Maine; but he soon made the acquaintance of the brethren here: and, though at first engaged for the greater part of the time in a neighboring field, he nevertheless so completely won their hearts by his gifts and his Christian simplicity, that, for years after he went back to his native State, they could not wean themselves from him.

On the first of July, 1814, he presided at the first business meeting of the church, where a vote was passed to raise five dollars "to purchase the elements for the use of the church for the ensuing year;" and Brother Jason Houghton was chosen Senior Deacon; Brother Ezra Tilden, Junior Deacon and Treasurer; and Brother Friend Crane, Clerk.(15)

* Life of Chaplain Fuller, p. 12 (*Walker and Wise*).

† Although the "Baptist Society" still existed, and continued in town affairs, and doubtless in the common talk of the towns-people, to be confounded with this church, yet the members of that organization, as such, never had any voice in the meetings of the Baptists after the formation of the church, or kept any records, or had any thing to do with the progress of the Baptist cause in Canton. The members of that body combined together simply for purposes of expediency, and continued to receive accessions for many years, of persons who wished to be exempted from paying the ministerial tax, but of whose names the records of this church are entirely ignorant. They are found upon the records of the town. The withdrawals from the old order became so numerous as to embarrass the parish in the maintenance of their minister. In 1820, Mr. Ritchie was, on this account, constrained to accept a considerable reduction of his salary.— *Old Parish Records*, vol. ii. p. 6.

Henry Kendall

In December (the 18th) also of the same year, he is mentioned in the records as moderator of a church-meeting;[(16)] and he was evidently here at different times during 1815 and 1816, perhaps 1817. His last visit to Canton was made in October, 1836, when the people heard once more his apostolic voice, and received his final benediction.*

Henry Kendall was born in Sanford, Me., July 3, 1774. His public studies were limited to three weeks' schooling, while apprenticed to the tanner's trade. He was converted in 1798, and, after working at his trade nearly three years, was licensed by the Baptist Church in Meredith, N.H., in the month of April, 1802. He received ordination at Mt. Vernon, Me., on the 5th of June, 1805, and labored as an itinerant preacher in his native State until 1812, when he was elected representative from Litchfield to the General Court at Boston. From an acquaintance formed with him then in that city, a liberal-minded Christian sister was induced to send for him two years afterwards, to labor at her expense in Sharon, where there had never been a revival of religion, and few or none were found to hold up the standard of evangelical Christianity. He complied with her request, and became, under God's blessing, the founder of the Baptist Church there. It was during his labors in Sharon, and a short time after, that he preached here: since then he has employed himself as an evangelist in different parishes of Maine, until, about ten years ago, an affection of the head unfitted him for labor. He still survives in China, of his native State, having extended his life into the last decade of a century.†

In September, 1814, the church received two by baptism, and adopted the following Constitution as a guide in the future transaction of business, and as a basis of discipline:—

WE, having found it to be our duty to give ourselves to one another in church fellowship, esteem it further to be our duty to govern ourselves by the rules given by the great Head of the Church; and that good order,

* Records Ladies' Benevolent Society, vol. i. p. 6.

† Life of Elder Henry Kendall, by himself (*Brown & Thurston*, Portland, 1853). He died in China, Me., Aug. 15, 1864.

peace and harmony may be maintained among us, we agree to the following articles; viz.: —

I. In all meetings of the church, the highest officer present shall preside; and if none be present, then one shall be chosen for the time being.

II. All church meetings shall be notified by the Moderator, with the advice of his brethren.

III. No complaint shall be brought into the church against any member, without the lower steps of labor first being taken, as described by our Saviour in Matthew, 18th chapter, 15th, 16th, and 17th verses; except the crime be of such a heinous nature as to demand the immediate exclusion of the member.

IV. No member shall be allowed to speak to any question before the church more than twice, without liberty of the church.

V. No member, when speaking, shall be interrupted by another, except it be to correct a mistake.

VI. Every vote passed by the church shall be accurately recorded by the Clerk.

VII. No candidate shall be admitted into the church to the destruction of the fellowship of one of its members; and all persons wishing for membership shall come before the church, and relate their experience; and, if any objection shall arise, the candidate shall be put by until the church shall examine into the nature of the objection. If the church shall judge the objection to be groundless, the objector shall submit it peaceably to the church, or suffer exclusion; then the candidate may be received, and good order will be maintained in the Church of Christ.

VIII. In any meeting of the church, any one of its members shall have a right to inquire after the spiritual health of any of its absent members, not intimating any thing like a complaint; and the church shall have a right to appoint a committee of inquiry to inquire after any of its absent members; and said committee shall report to the church, per order.

IX. No member, in presence of the church, shall implicate any one of its members; but, in case any matter in question shall be a burden to any member, it shall be his duty to inquire of the Moderator into its propriety; whose duty it shall be to call the attention of the church immediately to the subject.

X. In all questions before the church, a majority shall govern, except in the reception of members; but in all questions that have a tendency to divide the church, it must be governed by the discretion of the body.

XI. It shall be the established order of this church to hold a church conference on the Friday preceding the full of the moon, at 6 o'clock, P.M., except when the moon fulls on Friday. In such case, the meeting will be held on Friday, at the usual hour.*

XII. In the reception or dismissing of members, the sisters are to act; but in all matters of labor, they are not to act.

A code of Prudential Regulations was adopted in May,

* This rule of a monthly evening church-meeting, prior to communion, has been adhered to in the main particulars. In 1843, the attempt was made to fix the covenant-meeting in the *afternoon* (two o'clock); but the change did not operate well, and the old evening meeting was re-established. — *Church Records*, pp. 138, 150, 159.

1854, different from this in many essential particulars, having reference chiefly to officers and their duties.(195)

In 1814, the Warren Baptist Association included all the churches of the denomination in south-eastern Massachusetts and Rhode Island; and, as Canton fell within the limits, it was necessary for the new church to seek a formal union with that body. Accordingly, Elder Elisha Williams prepared a letter, which was copied, and sent by Brother Oliver Houghton to the meeting of the Association, in Providence.

In the mean time, the prospects of the country grew dark. In Canada, the American general, Wilkinson, had been defeated; Baltimore had been attacked, and many of her best citizens slain. The bloody battle of Niagara had been fought with but doubtful advantage to the American cause; and, worst of all, the capital of the nation was in the hands of a foreign enemy. Added to this, the victorious army that had fought in Europe under Wellington, and conquered Napoleon at Waterloo, had now quartered its thousands upon our frontier; and thus far the want of competent generals, and the partisan character of our measures of war, had tended rather to cripple our power of defence, until the country lay almost at the mercy of its invaders. It was "in view of these troubles now rolled upon the land" that the Association at its meeting, solemnly recommended to the churches to observe "Thursday, the 29th of September," as a day of fasting and prayer. It is the impression of the surviving original members, that that fast was observed by this church.

Forty names stood on the church-roll at the close of the year 1814. During the next year, the question of building a meeting-house began to be agitated.(16) The news of the return of peace * encouraged the little band of Christians to

* An ingenious old minor melody entitled "Retrospect, an Anthem from Sundry Scriptures," and written in this neighborhood just after the Revolution, now became popular again in singing-societies and family-gatherings. The following are its words:—

"Was not the day dark and gloomy?
The enemy said, 'Let us draw a line
even from York to Canada;'

But, praised be the Lord, the snare is
broken and we are escaped.
Hark! hear the adjuration:

venture more in their church expenditures, and some of their first essays in raising money are both entertaining and instructive. The following is a verbatim copy of a church vote recorded under date of Sept. 1, 1815: —

"Voted or appointed Br. F. Crane to get printed the church Articles of faith and Articles of regulation. Bro. Nathan Tucker subscribed to pay $\frac{1}{4}$ part the expense for printing,

Br. Dea^{n} Houghton,	$\frac{1}{4}$
Bro. Oliver Houghton,	$\frac{1}{8}$
Br. Friend Crane,	$\frac{1}{8}$
Br. Dea^{n} Tilden,	$\frac{1}{8}$
Br. Samuel Tucker,	$\frac{1}{16}$
Br. Lemuel Fuller,	$\frac{1}{16}$

We united in prayer with Dea^{n} Tilden. Our hearts were made glad and the meeting was closed. Expense of printing the above-named articles is $7.50.

Attest: F. CRANE, *Clerk*."[17]

We hear it said sometimes, that it is sacrilegious to mix religion with money; but those good brethren, now dead and gone, evidently exercised the spirit of prayer while they "subscribed to pay," and their "hearts were made glad."

No definite action in reference to building a meeting-house was taken at this early period, further than to "confer with

Cursed be the man that keepeth back
his sword!
O dismal! O horrible!
My bowels, my bowels!
I am pained at my very heart;
My heart maketh a noise within me;
For thou hast heard, O my soul, the
sound of the trumpet
And the alarm of war!
Behold my father! See my brother!
Hear him groan! See them die!
O thou sword of the Lord!
How long will it be ere that thou be quiet?
Put thyself into thy scabbard;
Rest, rest, and be still!
Cause us to hear with joy
Thy kind, inviting voice;
That so the bones which thou hast broke
May with fresh strength rejoice.
Hark! my soul, catch the sound!
Hear and rejoice!
Beat your swords into ploughshares,
And your spears into pruning-hooks,
And learn war no more.
How beautiful upon the mountains
Are the feet of him that bringeth good tidings;
That publisheth peace, —
Peace on earth, good-will towards men!
Hallelujah; for the Lord God omnipotent reigneth!
Hallelujah — Amen."

Mrs. Sherman,"* through a committee, with a view to securing a piece of land. It was the plan then to unite with the Randolph Church in building the house; and this accounts for the contemplated choice of a spot on "Mrs. Sherman's" land, in Ponkapog, close to where the fire-engine house now stands.

For preaching, the church at first depended mainly upon Elder Kendall, Elder Williams, and Bro. Ensign Lincoln, who took turns in the supply, with occasional assistance from others, until the spring of 1816.

About this time, the Lord was pleased to pour out his Spirit upon the church.† A great awakening came upon the whole region in March; and in the towns of Sharon, Easton, Foxboro', Mansfield, Attleboro', Bridgewater, Pawtucket, and Providence, believers were strengthened, and sinners flocked to Christ. In Canton, the people of God were greatly encouraged by the revival of their own graces and the conversion of souls. Apparently uncaused by the efforts of any preacher, a strong spiritual interest pervaded the community, and proved its divine origin, as a few years before, both by its hatefulness to the ungodly, and its fruits in the life of the church. Many went from house to house exhorting their neighbors to repent, and nothing seemed to be wanting but the labors of a judicious pastor to enable them to gather in a permanent and valuable harvest. Elder Kendall left about the first of March; and Bro. Lincoln, in consequence of his business, could spend little or no time here outside of the Sabbath. In their lack of a regular ministry, the church leaned much upon Elder Williams; and the nine or ten who joined the communion as the fruits of this first revival were baptized by his hands.

Of all the ministers who watched around the cradle of this church, none had so much to do with its early nurture and discipline as Elder Williams. At its very entrance into life,

* A family connection of Roger Sherman, of Revolutionary memory, who originally owned large real estate in this neighborhood. His father lies in the Canton Cemetery.

† Life of Elder Henry Kendall, p. 94.

he stood its god-father; and his interest in its measures and movements, for seven or eight years, was like that of Paul for his Macedonian converts. He presided at the constituting council; it was his wisdom, chiefly, that drafted the "Rules of Order" for the church; his pen wrote the first Associational Letter; and his lips pronounced the sermon and the prayer at the dedication of the first meeting-house. As his name transpires again in connection with this last service, a brief sketch of him will be given at that point in the history.

On the 26th of May, 1816, "Brother Leland Howard, of Vermont," * was unanimously invited to come here, and tarry "six months or a year, as would, in his opinion, be most usefull."(18) Bro. Howard had preached somewhat here, during the time of his study with Rev. James M. Winchell, of Boston (successor of Stillman, and compiler of the well-known "Winchell's Watts"); and the people being pleased with his spirit and gifts wished to hear him longer. He, however, declined the invitation; and, about a fortnight after, application was made to the Sharon Church to share with them alternately the ministrations of Elder John B. Gibson, of Newport, who was at that time supplying there. Bro. Gibson preached here three Sabbaths; but the church could not agree to any permanent arrangement with him,† and in August, Bro. GEORGE EVANS, of South Reading, was sent for.

The church now entered upon an experience of adversity, that, following so close upon the promise of the previous spring, was disheartening indeed. Overcome by the persecuting hostility of men of influence in the town, who carried the vulgar hatred of the Baptists to the extent of persecution, nearly every male member deserted his post, and left the deacons and the sisters alone.

* Still minister of the gospel in Rutland, in that State.

† Life of Elder Henry Kendall, p. 175. Elder John B. Gibson was an Arminian Methodist preacher, until the summer of 1802, when he was persuaded to Baptist views by a sermon of Elder John Peak. He died early in the year 1831. — *Memoir of Elder J. Peak, by himself.* Boston : 1832; pp. 135, 6, 7, 8.

George Evans

At last, about the middle of the fall, the enemies of the truth succeeded in shutting the little band of worshippers out of the North school-house where, up to that time, they had met unmolested as often as they chose.* This insult, however, was productive of more good than harm to the church. Bro. Friend Crane opened the large upper chamber of his dwelling-house † for religious meetings; and, so far from being silenced, the harassed believers prayed and praised with new inspiration, and cleaved more closely together.

Bro. Evans accepted, after a time, the invitation extended him by the church, and was here, probably in the winter, and certainly in the spring, of 1817, attaching himself very strongly to the church. George Evans was a good man; as a minister of Christ singularly faithful, devoted, and self-sacrificing. He was born in South Reading, Mass., Sept. 26, 1784; was licensed in the spring of 1809, and preached first in North Reading. After his brief term of labor in Canton, he removed West; but it is evident that the people here regarded him as their minister; and, while he was in the valley of the Mississippi, they sent him an urgent request to return and labor with them again. After an absence of several years, in the spring of 1823 he once more came to Canton, but made only a brief visit. In the summer of 1825, he made his home here, and preached alternately to this and Sharon church, until some time in the following spring. During this period, he became instrumental to the conversion of Francis Mason. He died in Manchester, N.H., Jan. 18, 1848.‡

After Bro. Evans's departure, there is some evidence that Elder Kendall visited this place again, and preached here and in the vicinity during the fore-part of the summer.§

* Life of Elder Henry Kendall, p. 175.

† The house opposite where the old meeting-house (town-house) stands, now enlarged, and used by Mr. James Draper in his manufacture of worsteds. Friend Crane's store was in the lower part of this house.

‡ Memoir of Elder George Evans, by his brother.

§ See a letter of Deacon Ezra Tilden (July 1, 1817), in Life of Elder Kendall p. 181.

After this the church had no regular ministerial supply until September, when Warren Bird,* a faithful young brother from Foxboro', came and preached three months.†

Probably but a small proportion of all the ministers who preached here prior to the erection of the meeting-house are mentioned in the Records, and doubtless some of them have passed entirely from the memory of the church. The aged members recollect the names of Coleman and Wheelock and Benson and Conant and Sawyer and N. W. Williams and Palmer and Judson and Chessman and Lovell and Waitt and Farley and Smith and Joy Handy, and Putnam the younger, and Otis Briggs, son of Elder Joel. Coleman was Rev. James, of the Eastern Missions, and, at the time of his preaching here, a member of Dr. Sharp's church. He sailed on Sunday, Nov. 16, 1817, for Burmah, and settled at Rangoon, where he died in 1822. Wheelock was Rev. Edward, the missionary, and the friend and associate of Coleman; when he preached here, he was a licentiate of Dr. Baldwin's church. He accompanied Coleman in 1817, but soon lost his health, and while *en route* for Bengal, intending to return home, he was drowned, Aug. 20, 1819.‡ Benson (Elder Caleb), of Middleboro', was known as "Blind Benson." He was an humble but gifted minister, and left grateful remembrances in Canton of his piety and faithfulness. Conant was Elder Thomas, well remembered as "Father Conant, of Abington." N. W. Williams, like Elder Elisha, was for a time pastor of the church of Beverly: B. W. Williams, of Boston, and Rev. N. M. Williams, of South Danvers, are his sons. Palmer was Elder William Palmer, of Connecticut: the church addressed him an invitation to come to Canton with a view to settlement; but his stay was short.§ Judson was Rev. Adoniram, father of Dr. Judson, the celebrated missionary. He was

* Rev. Warren Bird became a Swedenborgian in 1829, and died in Foxboro', Oct. 17, 1863. — *New Jerusalem Magazine*, xxxv. 362.

† Life of Elder Henry Kendall, pp. 98, 99.

‡ Knowles' Life of Ann H. Judson, pp. 135, 154; Baptist Magazine, vol. ii. pp. 263, 306; Life of Elder Henry Kendall, p. 99.

§ Life of Elder Kendall, p. 93.

pastor of a Congregational church in Plymouth, but became a Baptist after his son's arrival in Burmah. He related while in Canton, that, on hearing the news of Adoniram's conversion to Baptist views, he walked his chamber twelve days and nights, finding no rest. He was a stern old man, and little accustomed to allow his belief to be questioned; and when we consider the denominational hostility prevalent in 1811 and thereabouts, between Congregationalists and Baptists, his agitation is not wonderful. He, however, searched the Scriptures, and, having satisfied himself in the very views which his son had embraced, was baptized, with his wife and daughter, by Dr. Baldwin. He died in Scituate, Nov. 25, 1826, aged 76.* Rev. Daniel Chessman was a worthy Boston minister of the old school, a friend of Dr. Baldwin, and subsequently author of a memoir of him. Rev. Samuel Waitt was the pastor of the Sharon church,† ordained there June 3, 1818;(21) but he occasionally filled the Canton pulpit as well as his own. The two churches drew kindly together, being of the same age, and neighbors; and it was much the custom in their early days to accommodate each other in their pastoral supplies.

In the year 1817 occurred the first case of extreme discipline. Between January and October, three were excluded from fellowship; all of them being constituent members. The church, however, received some additions by baptism, and at the close of the year numbered forty-eight. The demand for a permanent place of worship had by this time become imperative. Four years of rotary life had proved the patience, as well as the cohesiveness, of the church; and now, the sparrow must have a house, the swallow a nest for herself, where she might lay her young. After much prayer and careful thought, and many close counsels, at length, in the early part of September, 1818, the gathering of contributions commenced; (22) and, before the end of the following month, the plan of

* Wayland's Life of Judson, vol. i. p. 13.

† Min. Bost. So. Assoc. 1853. Mr. Waitt removed South, and became president of a female college in South Carolina. At last accounts of him, he was still resident there.

the meeting-house was drawn, and all the necessary committees appointed, not forgetting the one to keep the subscription-paper in circulation. The Ponkapog lot had been abandoned, and a site had been fixed upon in Otis Billings' land, that "corners on the Taunton and Dedham Roads," opposite to where Mr. James Sumner now lives; but, failing to procure this, the church had purchased of Alexander French, for eighty dollars, a building spot on the opposite side of the "Taunton (Boston) Road," about eighty rods south-east of the old grave-yard, in the centre of the town. The foundation of the house was laid in 1819; but the work did not reach completion until the latter part of the next year.

Meantime, the church, though suffering many inconveniences, continued to meet and observe the ordinances. Up to Aug. 30, 1820, it would seem that they had been somewhat irregular in the observance of the Lord's Supper; though by the 11th article of their constitution (p. 20) it was evidently their intention to hold that sacrament monthly; but, on the day above named, it was voted [25] to celebrate it "on the last Lord's Day in every other month:" subsequently the time was changed to the first Sabbath in every month, as it still continues to be.

By a strange neglect, no record of the dedication of the meeting-house is made upon the church book. Aged people remember only that Elder Elisha Williams preached the sermon, and made the dedicatory prayer; that the Unitarian choir assisted at the services; and that a *snow-storm* raged the whole day. The following notice, however, of the dedication, communicated very likely by Elder Williams himself, appears in the old Baptist Magazine: * —

"The new meeting-house in Canton, erected the past season by the Baptist church and society in that place, was opened on Lord's Day, Jan. 14 (1821), by the solemn and delightful worship of God. The sermon was preached by Rev. Elisha Williams, founded on 2 Chron. 7th chapter and 1st verse: 'Now, when Solomon had made an end of praying, the fire came down from heaven, and consumed the burnt-offering and the sacrifices; and the

* Vol. vii. p. 80.

Elisha Williams.

glory of the Lord filled the house.' The pleasing circumstances under which this house was opened inspire the hope that it will continue to be a sanctuary in which the pure principles of the gospel will be vindicated, and their holy tendency enforced on those who, in the present and future generations, may meet there for social worship; that the glory of the Lord, in the power of the gospel on the hearts of sinners, and in the enjoyment of his presence, may encourage the exertions of the church in the cause for which their Redeemer bled. And thus may it be apparent that their labor was not in vain in the Lord!"

The prayer of Elder Williams on this occasion is remembered from an exclamation of one of the auditory at the time, "He prayed like an angel!" This good man appears here for the last time (but one*) in connection with the history of this church. Many fields of New England's Zion besides our own preserve grateful remembrances of his useful life.

ELISHA SCOTT WILLIAMS was born in East Hartford, Ct., Oct. 7, 1757, of Congregational stock. He graduated at Yale College, in 1775, when only eighteen years old, and served in the Revolution as adjutant in a Connecticut regiment,† and on board the privateer "Hancock." After the war, he lived in Stockbridge, Mass., about ten years, and removed to Maine, where he taught school, and was elected a justice of the peace. About 1798, while residing at Livermore, Me., he was converted to God, and soon after licensed there to preach the gospel. He was ordained in August, 1799, by the Bowdoinham Association, and soon became pastor of the Baptist Church in Brunswick, where he labored till 1803, when he was settled over the First Baptist Church in Beverly, Mass. He remained there till 1812, and then removed to Boston. After a residence of twenty-five years in that city, he returned to Beverly, and died there Feb. 3, 1845. In his person, Elder Williams was tall and stately; in manners, grave; vehement on occasion; a gentleman of the old school. In the pulpit, he was solemn and impressive, but oftener didactic than glowing.

* See page 40.

† While serving in the army, he crossed the Delaware with Washington as one of the general's aids. In John Trumbull's well-known picture of that eventful stratagem, the portrait of Williams, introduced from life by the artist, is plainly discernible.

Elder Williams published during his life a Dialogue on Baptism, and a sermon in the "Baptist Preacher." * Fragments remembered here at this day, and recited with veneration when his life and services are talked of, show that he was wont to drop philosophical sayings, and sometimes indulged in verse. Among other things, he used to say, "There is nothing that we can want but what God has promised, and there is nothing that he has promised which we do not want;" and, in reference to allowing impertinent thoughts to disturb worship, he used quaintly to remark, "Although we cannot hinder the birds from flying over our heads, we may prevent their roosting in our hair." The following lines are part of a poem written by him on his seventy-second birthday: —

"Hail once again, auspicious morn
On which poor helpless I was born
To pleasure and to pain!
Of both, forsooth, I've had my share,
For, duly mixed, they cure despair,
And vain desires restrain.

. . . . . .

Threescore and twelve revolving years,
With all their joys and griefs and fears,
I speedily have passed, &c."

Our first church edifice, consecrated by the prayers of Elder Williams, stands now where it was originally built, and with scarcely an alteration from its original fashion, — a plain structure, without steeple or porch, forty feet long by thirty-six wide, fronting the south. Its cost was about two thousand dollars.

Mr. Leonard Everett appears to have been the first sexton (so far as there was any). †(74) Probably at first the doors were not so thronged as to render his duties very burdensome.‡ Afterwards, as the congregation increased, we find "Brother

* Christian Watchman, Feb. 14, 1845; Sprague's Annals Am. (Bap.) Pulpit, pp. 392–94.

† Mr. Everett was a member of the Unitarian Society.

‡ Although many had withdrawn from the standing order, these seceders were not all meeting-goers. The population of the town, too, always subject to fluctuations, was

Enos Upham appointed to wait upon strangers who may attend our meeting from time to time, and furnish them with seats," — an excellent and most politic provision always, to say nothing of the Christianity of it. Often the size of a Sabbath

congregation depends less upon the preacher than upon the manner in which the ushers magnify their office.

While the house was building, the people listened for a time to the preaching of Rev. Edmund Billson, an Englishman. He was an able speaker; but some rash expressions uttered by him in his discourses made them so out of conceit with him, that they refused to allow him to minister in their new sanctuary, and he left them to return no more.

All debts and demands against the church, on account of their building, were promptly paid or compounded. A choir was organized; and Elder THOMAS BARRETT, who had occasionally officiated before in the parish,[(26)] was invited[(27)] to divide his ministerial labors between Canton and Sharon, receiving as his portion from this half of his "diocese" one hundred and fifty dollars for one year. He continued to reside in Sharon, where he had been laboring for some time already;

not such as to warrant a great Sunday congregation. Indeed, the census of the previous year showed that the number of inhabitants in Canton had *decreased* nearly a hundred since 1810.

but, during the year 1821, this church counted him her pastor.

In June of the same year, a Sunday school was added to the other means of grace;[28] Deacon Ezra Tilden being appointed the first superintendent. The Baptist Sunday school in Canton really began eight or ten years before, in the Old North School-house, at which place a few faithful men and women were wont to gather with their children on Sabbath days to study the Bible and Catechism; but there seems to have been little or no organization to their efforts until the above date.

The church numbered but forty-five at the time they entered their new house of worship. In the spring of 1819, they had numbered fifty; but, during that year and the next, three were dismissed to Randolph, and two died. During Elder Barrett's ministry, some were added, both by baptism and by letter; but, several cases of severe discipline occurring, the membership of the church was reduced in a year and a half to forty-three. The fathers meant to guard well the heritage of God, and were not often chargeable with slighting their work; yet those who criticise the strictness of the older Baptists, and complain (no doubt in some cases justly) of the harshness of the early discipline of the church, will be surprised at a letter of dismission, bearing date June 3, 1822, which certifies "that our beloved sister Mary Hunt is a member in good standing in the Baptist Church in Canton; and, upon her request, we dismiss her, to unite with the Methodist Church in Boston, hoping that she will continue to honor the cause of the dear Redeemer."[34]

Elder Barrett left his charge here in the spring of 1822. He was a preacher of much power, generally choosing short, pithy texts, and using with great effect those passages of Scripture which are best adapted to awaken the conscience. His prevailing temper of piety, however, was gloomy; and, being very self-depreciative and distrustful, he failed to derive the proper vigor and hopefulness from the love of Jesus. This disposition produced deep religious melancholy, and finally insanity, which terminated in suicide. He ended his days in

Webster, Aug. 7, 1832, aged only forty years, having been born in Woodstock, Ct., Aug. 27, 1792. He studied for the ministry with the Rev. Antipas Steward, Rev. David Pease, and Rev. Thomas Rand, and was ordained in Grafton, June 12, 1816, making his term of pastoral labor sixteen years. There remains no portrait of him. He is described as tall and portly, with an impressive personal presence, and a complexion inclining to sandy.

Thomas Barrett

The Baptists were now once more destitute of a stated ministry. Sensible of their need of the labors of a settled pastor, they made an effort to raise a sufficient sum of money to support one, and, by the first of June, they were able to offer three hundred dollars. "Elder Houghton, of Winthrop," was first invited to "preach on trial;" but no engagement was effected with him, and the people contented themselves with chance supplies and alternate supplies till the following spring. Among the various preachers who dispensed the word here during the year 1822, the one who made his mark most decidedly of all was Bro. Thomas Ford, of Boston, the father of Daniel S. Ford, Esq., Editor of the "Christian Watchman and Reflector." He was a native Englishman, a prominent member of Dr. Sharp's church, and, like Ensign Lincoln, a licensed layman. Dr. Wayland, who was ever known to be a champion of lay-preaching, often referred to Bro. Ford, whom he heard in his younger days, as a noble instance of the efficiency of unordained talent in the pulpit.* In the

* A testimony equally significant and valuable to the power and unction of Brother Thomas Ford, as a preacher, came from a colored barber, who told how often he used to walk through the spring slush, to Charles Street, from the extreme North End, to hear him talk in evening meetings.

As a sample of the quaint way in which he was wont to fortify his utterances with texts of Scripture, it is related, that on one occasion, when a young, and not very promising candidate preached before Dr. Sharp's church for a license, he was called upon, after an embarrassing silence at the close of the sermon, to give his opinion in

spring of 1823, Elder George Evans, their beloved evangelist, made the people a visit,[(35)] on his return from the West, and preached among them, much to the joy and reviving of their hearts.

Bro. Henry Stanwood, a young licentiate, next supplied the pulpit for some time, and his labors proved very acceptable and useful. During his stay, the church was blessed, souls were converted, and, in the summer and fall of 1823, fourteen were received into the communion; Elders Benjamin Putnam, of Randolph, and Joseph Eliot, of Roxbury, administering the ordinance of baptism. This was the second revival in the church.

Elder Eliot was a preacher of considerable note at that day, possessed of a good person, engaging manners, and excellent oratorical powers. Being unhappy in his settlement, he frankly told the church in Canton that he would be glad to become their pastor. Many felt an inclination to settle him here; but that was finally overruled, partly by special reasons existing in the minds of the people, and partly by his own subsequently changed views of the matter. Observing to them that an extended field would better suit him than this "small garden," he turned their attention to Rev. FORRIS MOORE, a young "up-country" clergyman, whom he had baptized, as being a fit person to serve them in the ministry, he having a much smaller family, and health sufficient only for limited labors. The result was, that Elder Moore came to Canton, and Elder Eliot moved into his place, at New Ipswich, N.H.*

This year the church, upon request, was dismissed from the old Warren Association, and joined the Boston Association. Aid had been received from abroad at different times, in support of the Baptist cause in the place; and record is made this

the case, and expressed himself as follows: "I believe the young brother to be a very good man; but, if I were to advise him as to his entering the ministry, I should say to him much as Eli said to Samuel, 'Go and lie down, my son, till the Lord calleth thee.'"

* The same conveyance that brought the goods of one carried away the goods of the other. It was remarked in a pleasant way by one of the sisters here that "Mr. Eliot unseated Mr. Moore, and sat down in his chair."

Horris Moore

summer of a vote of thanks to the Norfolk Domestic and Foreign Mission Society, and also to certain liberal brethren in the town of Randolph, for sums of money forwarded in the interest of this church.[37, 38]

Elder Moore commenced his labors here on the 19th of July, 1824.* When he came to the church, there were fifty-five communicants in it, and four were added by baptism during his stay of about a year. He was compelled by feeble health to resign his charge, and left Canton in June, 1825. This faithful and suffering minister was born in Putney, Vt., Dec. 31, 1796. He indulged a hope in Christ when thirteen years of age, but did not profess religion till the summer of 1816, when he was baptized in Rockingham, of his native State, by Elder Eliot, who was then pastor of the Baptist Church there. After this he studied at Phillips' Academy, Andover, Mass., and while there his system was prostrated by two severe attacks of illness, which left him an invalid for life. He was ordained at Keene, N.H., Dec. 30, 1819, at which place, and at New Ipswich, of the same State, he performed the duties of a pastor until his settlement over this church. He died in South Lee, April 7, 1858. He ardently loved the work of the ministry, and honored the calling by his devout and godly life. His mind was clear and well balanced, and his heart, whether interested as a minister, a husband and father, or as a citizen and a Christian, was always warm and true. He labored in pain; but his almost forty years of tearful seed-sowing yielded him many sheaves. He is said to have been the first Baptist preacher in Canton who used notes.

Rev. Oren Tracy, of Randolph, was next called to the pastorate here, but never came otherwise than as an occasional supply; and the return of Elder George Evans occurring in the following August, the people enjoyed the welcome ministrations of a beloved former evangelist until spring.

The records of the year 1826 are a mournful memorial of

* He lived in the large old yellow house behind the two great willow-trees, at Canton Corner, still known as "the old Haynes House," and which continued to be a sort of parsonage for several years.

suspensions, expulsions, and death. The church enjoyed preaching only on alternate Sundays until fall, when, on the 15th of September, Elder SAMUEL ADLAM, an Englishman, was "unanimously and affectionately" called from Dedham. He remained here through the fall and winter; and it was at his hands that Francis Mason, now Dr. Mason, the distinguished Karen Missionary, received baptism.

The subsequent career of Mason, and his prominence in the Christian world, render it proper that he should receive a special notice in this history, even aside from the fact of his connection with this church. Francis Mason was born in York, England, April 2, 1799. At the age of nineteen, he availed himself of the offer of an uncle in America to pay his passage hither, and landed in Philadelphia in May, 1818. His uncle took him to Cincinnati, but died there soon after, leaving him a stranger and alone. He became a wanderer, and for nearly six years roamed up and down in Ohio, Kentucky, Indiana, Illinois, Missouri, and Mississippi, "living without an object." While staying at Natchez, he rejected a good opportunity to acquire a medical education, believing it better, he said, "to be a good shoemaker" (which he already was) "than to be a bad doctor." At length, while on a visit to New Orleans, he saw a ship bound to Boston, and immediately engaged a passage in her. He arrived in Boston in the summer of 1824, and remained in that city about a year; but his life there, according to his own testimony, was wretched, aimless, and unhappy. Like Judson, he became a frequenter of playhouses, and having tried these, with nearly every other variety of diversion, without any satisfaction to himself, he came to feel that his very existence was a gift not worth the having. One day, while in this state of mind, he said laughingly to some of his associates, "I will go into the country, become religious, and settle down for life in the Bay State." The careless remark proved partly prophetic; and the year 1825 found him in Randolph, surrounded by the very influences which were to make him a faithful and efficient servant of God. He boarded in the family of Elder Benjamin Putnam, and followed his trade of boot-making. Elder Putnam was faithful to set before him the importance of religion, and urge upon him the necessity of a change of heart. He was sceptical, but took instruction kindly, and through the influence of Miss Lucinda Gill, a young woman of earnest piety, and a member of this church,* who resided in Elder Putnam's family, and to whom he became devotedly attached, he began to read and study the Bible. Subsequently (in December, 1825) he married Miss Gill, and removed to Canton, where he boarded in the family of Deacon Tilden. His study of the Bible was faithfully continued. At his hours of work, he would place the holy book in the open drawer of his work-bench, where his eye could catch the words; and, when a visitor entered the shop, he would push the drawer in.

This honest perusal of the Scriptures, with the immediate effect of the kind exhortations of Rev. George Evans,† brought him at last, in the early part of the year 1826, to the light of a joyful hope in Christ. Spots in the woods, neighboring to the old Tilden homestead, bear witness, this day, to the fervor of Mason's first prayers. Thoroughly interested now in the matter of the gospel, he spared no pains to put himself in the way of listening to its teachings; and on Sabbath days, when there was no preaching in Canton, he often walked with Deacon Tilden to Dedham.‡ There he became acquainted with Bro. Adlam, and his preaching, his nearness of age, and the strong attraction of a common nationality, drew Mason towards him in deep and lasting friendship. There is little doubt but it was Mason who procured his call to Canton. The future missionary was baptized in Reservoir Pond, a little above Pleasant Street, in the month of October, 1826; being the first candidate to whom young Adlam ever administered this Christian rite. At the same time, he received the hand of fellowship to this church, in whose communion he still remains. Surprising as it may

* See page 21.

† Memoir of Elder George Evans, p. 52; Mason's Autograph Reminiscences.

‡ West Dedham.

seem, no record of this transaction was made on the church-book; neither was Mason's name ever entered on the church-roll. Were it not that the parties are still living, the facts and dates would probably never have been verified.

Immediately after his conversion, Mason's soul was fired with the zeal of an evangelist. He would go to India, and he set himself at once to study for a preparation. Elder Adlam taught him the Greek and Hebrew alphabet, sitting beside him on the shoe-bench; and he afterwards took lessons in the Greek classics, two or three times a week, of Mr. Huntoon, the pastor of the Unitarian Church. He was licensed here on the 1st of October, 1827, and, after two years of theological study at Newton,* was ordained by the Baldwin-place Church, Boston, May 23, 1830. The next day he set sail, with Kincaid, for Calcutta.†

F. Mason

Mrs. Mason died here, soon after her husband's graduation at Newton.‡ She was an excellent woman, and her husband trusted in her. He testifies, "She had much to do, in God's providence, with my conversion. Blessings on her memory!" She left a little son, a fine, promising boy, to the care of her sister Abigail (now Mrs. Capen, of West Bridgewater). With her faithful attentions the child thrived, and bade fair to grow up an honor and a joy to his devoted father, and to the cause whose sacrifices had been his first inheritance. As appears

* His graduating essay (1829) was entitled "The Man of Sin."

† Baptist Magazine, vol. xiv. pp. 409–10.

‡ She died Nov. 18, 1829, aged thirty-three. Her first infant, Wayland Putnam, died two years before in Milton, aged one year and eleven months.

S. Adlam.

from letters written at that date,* Mr. Mason had set his heart on his being a missionary, and succeeding him in Burmah; but God willed it otherwise. Disease set in at the time he was vaccinated; and he sank under it, in spite of all the love and vigilance of his nurse, being only two years old when he died. Rev. Lucius Bolles, D.D., then Secretary of the American Baptist Missionary Union, came from Boston, and officiated at his funeral, Jan. 12, 1831, at the residence of his aunt, the house now owned by the Blake heirs, and standing on the north side of Pleasant Street, about a quarter of a mile east of Reservoir Pond. A little mound close to the grave of his mother, in the cemetery in Canton, now covers the child of promise, — the dust of Francis Wayland Mason.

Elder Adlam left this people early in 1827. He was born in Bristol, Eng., Feb. 4, 1798; and was well acquainted with Dr. Ryland, and knew Foster, Jay, and Robert Hall. He studied with Dr. Wayland, then pastor of the First Baptist Church, Boston, and, some years after his pastorate in Canton, completed a theological education at Newton. He still lives, and preaches in Newport, R.I.

After his departure, dismissions, deaths, and discipline again reduced the members of the church; and, by August of this year, there were but forty-eight upon the roll. Previous to this date, however, they had secured a pulpit supply in the person of Brother Moses Curtis, — a young man from Providence, of modest manners and evident piety. As early as April, a letter was sent to Elder Stephen Gano to inquire "respecting his moral and religious character;" and the strong recommendation of this good man, seconded by their own knowledge of his worth,† determined the church to ordain him. They made arrangements to do so on the 29th of August. Meantime they fixed the salary of Brother Curtis at three hundred and fifty dollars, moved his furniture to Canton, and

* Letters from F. Mason to Miss Nabby Gill, Oct. 22, 1830; Nov. 3, 1830; Nov. 2, 1831.

† Being a native of East Stoughton, and acquainted with all the Baptists of Canton from his boyhood, Mr. Curtis had given the church ample opportunity to know him, and form a correct estimate of his character.

received him and his wife into church-fellowship. At the time of his ordination, he had supplied the church nearly four months. At the ordaining-services, on the 29th of August, Rev. James D. Knowles preached the sermon, and Elder Elisha Williams offered the ordaining prayer; the charge to the candidate was given by Elder Gano, his former pastor; Rev. Oren Tracy proffered the hand of fellowship; and Elder Benjamin Putnam, of North Randolph, gave the charge to the people.[(51)] No more interesting services had been witnessed in the new meeting-house since it was opened for worship. Brother Curtis commenced his pastorate, with a flock few in number, and feeble in means; but they were united in him, and the faith of both minister and people made them strong together.

A project, which had for a good while occupied the minds of the church, for raising a permanent fund of two thousand dollars to aid in the support of preaching among them, assumed this year the form of a church-vote. Assurances of help had been received by the members from friends abroad, which justified them in believing that they could now raise this sum if they chose to make the effort; and accordingly, on the 14th of September, 1827, Jason Houghton, Ezra Tilden, Friend Crane, Nathan Tucker, Samuel Tucker, Francis Mason, and Clifford Belcher, were chosen a committee to solicit subscriptions. By July of the next year, the two thousand dollars was raised; and the church loaned it to the Second Baptist (or Baldwin Place) Church, Boston, then under the pastoral charge of Dr. Knowles. Their yearly interest from this loan, added to their other income for the support of the ministry, made out the voted salary of three hundred and fifty dollars. In the burning of Deacon Tilden's house some time afterwards, the note for this deposit was destroyed; but the church procured its renewal.[(63)]

The labors of Brother Curtis were soon blessed; and, during the year 1828, he had the happiness of baptizing six converts. In the following year, thirteen received the sacred seal at his hands; and in every thing the Lord seemed to bear wit-

Moses Curtis

ness to the fidelity of his ministry. A very interesting Bible-class of thirty members, besides forty younger learners of the word of God, assembled every Sunday in the Sabbath school; and the letter to the Association, for 1829, reported the church "awaking under the influences of the Holy Spirit." The church is also credited seventy-seven dollars this year for benevolent objects.*

But, with all this, Brother Curtis did not receive sufficient salary to support him. There was no wealth in the church; and, with all their willingness, the people probably went to the extent of their ability when they raised two hundred dollars outside of their fund. Besides, in the latter part of his ministry, the stoppage of the Stone Factory, taking away, as it did, nearly five hundred from the population of the town,† diminished Brother Curtis's congregation, and rendered the burden heavier upon those who remained to maintain him. Under date of April 27, 1829, there is this vote: "That the salary of Brother Curtis be three hundred and fifty dollars; and that he have the liberty of being absent a sufficient length of time to obtain fifty dollars, in addition to the above salary, by laboring elsewhere.[(58)]‡

But the spring of 1830 opened, and the days of his pastorate in Canton drew to a close. His last handwriting in the book of records is dated April; and in June he and his wife are written as members of the church in Medfield. MOSES CURTIS was born in East Stoughton, Mass., July 2, 1795, and converted to Christ at the age of seventeen. He studied Latin and Greek in a grammar-school, in Providence, and afterwards with Rev. Charles Train, of Framingham; and was licensed to preach by the First Baptist Church in Providence. He now resides in Belchertown.§

The membership of the Canton Church was now sixty-four.

* Baptist Magazine, xiii. 216, 392.

† In 1837, there were two hundred and fifty operatives, half male and half female, in Canton Woollen Mills. — *Hist. Coll. Mass.*

‡ He preached in Sharon, and got the fifty dollars.

§ He visited this place, and preached, Oct. 16, 1864.

Of this number, two young men, Charles Johnson, and Joseph Hodges, jun., were looking forward to the ministry; and, in December of this year, the church licensed the former to preach the gospel.[(70)] Brother Johnson was a son of Mr. Lewis Johnson, of Stoughton, who lately died at the advanced age of ninety-six. He received a theological education at Newton, and settled about the year 1835 in Maine, where he died. Brother Hodges, now also deceased, was licensed by this church in April, 1831.[(73)] He was also educated at Newton. He resided with his father at the Stone Factory, in this village, until 1835, when he removed to Roxbury. As pastor at Newton Upper Falls, at East Brookfield, and Three Rivers, and, later, as Agent of the American and Foreign Bible Society, he was long familiar by name to the Christian public, and useful in the vineyard of the Lord.

After the dismissal of Pastor Curtis, the reader of the church-records enters upon another unsettled period, abounding in reports of special discipline, and confused with a multiplicity of clerical names; showing that the church, whatever may be said of the wisdom of its course, was at least not inactive, and that the means of grace were not neglected. The movement of the church at this time[(68)] to unite with Sharon in procuring a half-way ministry, after the old plan, does not give satisfactory evidence of progress; and indeed the church-letter for the year 1830 reports the state of religion "low." It appears certain, nevertheless, that the *missionary spirit* of the people, and their disposition to give to benevolent objects, was this year, and for a considerable time before and after, in advance of any thing exhibited here during all the earlier or later history of the church. There were then special reasons for this which cannot always exist; but it is due that the fact should be recorded.

Shortly after the embarkation of Mason, in May, Dr. Bolles, Secretary of the Missionary Union, came and preached here once or twice; and Elder Seth Ewer, now of Norton, supplied the pulpit a while in the summer of this year. It was at about this period, too, that young William Hague, now Dr. Hague, of Boston, visited the place as a student minister from Newton, and preached among the people with a power that gave promise of his future fame. Occasionally, also, the voices of the young brethren, Johnson and Hodges, prophets not without honor even in their own country, were heard in exhortation both in pulpit and in private house.

Newton Theological Institution was at that time regarded with much interest and affection by the church, as was natural to them, having two licentiates studying there. There is an acknowledgment for Nov. 23, 1831, of "seven bed-quilts and comforters, two pairs of sheets, and one pair of pillow-cases," from Canton.* The institution was then in its infancy,† and supported to a large extent in this manner by the contributions of the churches. Mention has already been made of the charities of this church in 1829. Of these, twenty-four dollars were given to the Baptist Education Society to prepare young men for the ministry. It was a time of general solicitude on this subject; ‡ and it should be a cause of gratitude to us that our predecessors here were participants, to some extent, in the pious movement that has wrought so much good. The old Education Society, co-eval with our church, was the mother of the Baptist institutions of learning in Waterville, Hamilton, Newton, and Rochester. §

In December, 1830, one formerly excluded member was restored; and, in the spring of 1831, the church began to receive additions by baptism. The records had now become so deranged through the successive changes of years, that it was found necessary to revise them. According to their showing, the number of members was sixty; whereas the minutes of the Association gave seventy, very naturally provoking the wonder where they got their annual returns. ‖ At a meeting

* Baptist Magazine, vol. xvi. 223.

† Incorporated February, 1826.

‡ Baptist Magazine, xv. 46.

§ Watchman and Reflector, Nov. 10, 1864.

‖ Probably the habit of taking the *minutes of the preceding year* as a basis, and reckoning the desired additions or subtractions upon these, served to increase the error as it ran on through successive seasons.

in March of this year, held at Bro. Clifford Belcher's, a committee appointed to correct the list reported that the actual number then in the communion was but fifty-nine; and the roll was amended accordingly. At the same time, we find Bro. Nathan Tucker authorized to let the meeting-house to the town, to hold town-meetings in.(72)

A church-library had been formed some time previous to this; and, at about this date, we find Bro. Lemuel Tilden chosen librarian. Libraries in all the churches, "for the use of the minister and members," had been strongly recommended by the Association as early as 1823, and the recommendation was printed in the minutes for this and the three following years. It was urged in their favor, that they might prevent many a penniless pastor from falling into contempt for lack of general knowledge, and save the youth "from the ill effects of reading novels and romances." The books of the Canton Church-library were kept at the meeting-house in a book-case, and members of the church and congregation who wished to read them applied on Sunday for such as they liked. Bro. Henry Fisher was the next librarian, and held the office six years; after which, Sister Louisa Tucker had charge of the books for a short time. The library continued to receive additions until about 1840, when it became the property of the Sunday School. The following volumes, still preserved, are specimens of the old collection, —

Robinson's History of Baptism; 8vo.

Josephus's Works; 8vo.

Hist. of the Danish Mission to Coromandel, by Baron Stow; 12mo.

Means of a Revival, by J. Howard Hinton; 12mo.

The Telescope, by Samuel C. Nott; 12mo.

Life of John Newton, by W. B. Tappan; 12mo.

Life of Isabella Graham, by Divie Bethune; 12mo.

Memoir of Levi Parsons, by Chauncy Goodrich; 12mo.

Scougal's Works, published by Thurston, Boston; 12mo.

Davies's Sermons, published by Lincoln and Edmonds; 12mo.

On Friday, the 29th of April, 1831, a series of religious meetings was commenced in the meeting-house, first daily, then tri-weekly and semi-weekly; and an interest was awakened in the community, which continued for several months, and was productive of lasting good. Thirty-two were welcomed to the fellowship of the church, by baptism, between March and December. The preachers were many and various during that revival. We hear of Elders Peak and Clealand and Chase,* and Daniel Merrill and Caleb Green,† and Thomas and Joseph Driver,‡ and James Coley and Hiram Gear. Of these, as among the apostles of Jesus, one proved a wolf in sheep's clothing. John Clealand was a man of remarkable gifts. His commanding presence and popular address, and his rare talent in revival-singing, drew multitudes to the meetings when he preached, and captivated not a few into his confidence. Friends of the church from abroad, who knew his corrupt character, exposed him as soon as they learned of his stay here; and he was ignominiously sent away, after having deceived the people for nearly five months. He baptized six converts. On the very day of his apprehension for immorality and false pretences, he preached from Luke v. 26, "We have seen strange things to-day,"—a text considered quite significant by both the friends and the enemies of religion.

Elder John Peak was a member of Baldwin-place Church, Boston, and often served as a home missionary.§ He was born in Walpole, N.H., ‖ Sept. 26, 1761, and learned the tailor's trade. On the 18th of June, 1788, he was ordained at Windsor, Vt.; and subsequently preached much in Eastern New Hampshire and Massachusetts. He was best known as pastor of the church in Newburyport, where he labored from 1805 to

* Rev. Johnson Chase, of Boston.

† Rev. Caleb Green was minister at Sharon at that time.

‡ Of these two preachers, Elder *Thomas* Driver was oftenest and longest here, though the name of Elder Joseph only appears in the records.

§ Baptist Magazine, vols. xii.–xix.

‖ His parents were Congregationalists, and came from Woodstock and Ashford, Conn.

1818.* He lived to be an old man, and very lame, and was long known as "Father Peak."

Elder Daniel Merrill was settled as a Congregational minister in Sedgwick, Me., towards the close of the last century. He became a Baptist in 1804, and was baptized in the following year by Dr. Baldwin; a majority of his church at the same time following his example.†

The office of junior deacon having been vacant for more than a year by the resignation of Bro. Ezra Tilden, a church fast was appointed for the third Thursday in May, in view of the necessity of a new election. The meeting was held, and the lot fell upon Friend Crane.

For some time after the departure of Elder Clealand (in June), the Baptists realized little but sorrow and discouragement. The scandal caused by his treachery to truth and duty was deeply felt by them; but they soon rallied, and the work of the Lord, under the conduct of faithful helpers, went prosperously on. The associational letter for the year reports the church "in a peaceful and pleasant state." From July to September, Rev. James Madison Coley supplied the pulpit and administered the ordinances. Some of those who then received baptism at his hands, are this day among the most reliable members of the church.

In October, Brother Hiram Gear, who had already labored here for more than a month, was invited to preach for the church "so long as they could be useful to each other." His remuneration was to be "five dollars for each Lord's Day, and board," — terms, considering the last article particularly, which many a poor pastor would now be only too glad to comply with. It was during his stay here that a box of considerable size and value was sent, filled with comforts, to Dr.

* Memoir of Elder J. Peak, by himself. (Boston, 1832.)

† Sixty-six candidates, in all, were baptized then, including Mr. Merrill, who was baptized by Elder Baldwin, and Mrs. Merrill, who was baptized by Elder Williams. The whole ceremony occupied but forty-two minutes.—*Christian Watchman, Feb.* 14, 1845. At this rate (allowing each administrator three minutes to a candidate), the twelve apostles and the "other seventy" would have been about an hour and three-quarters baptizing the "three thousand."—*Maine Baptists*, pp. 263–6.

Mason, the missionary. It was made up mostly by the ladies of the church and society, and contained, — besides valuable clothing for himself, his wife and children, — books, dried apples, arrowroot, soap, and useful medicines, amounting, in all, to over thirty dollars. The box was sent early in the spring of 1832.*

Brother Gear remained with the church a little more than a year; at the close of which time, though earnestly requested to remain, he went elsewhere, to enter upon the work of an evangelist. To this service he was ordained here, at his desire, on the 11th of April, 1832; a council of ministers and delegates from Boston, Newton, Abington, Randolph, Sharon, Medfield, and Stoughton, having examined and approved him.

Hiram Gear was born in Middletown, Conn., May 6, 1804. Converted in 1825, he joined the Baptist church in his native place, and soon after received a license there, and pursued a course of preparatory study. He entered the Theological School at Newton in the fall of 1828, where he continued till his call to Canton. His labors, after leaving this place, were in Ohio, in the service of the Baptist Home Missionary Society; and he continued to be thus employed till his death, in the prime of his days, at Marietta, Feb. 20, 1843. He was an indefatigable worker, and a preacher of considerable power. In person he was tall and slender, his complexion dark, with eyes remarkably full and expressive, and an energetic manner that won attention, and carried conviction to the heart. No portrait of him is preserved.

H. Gear

The occasion of Brother Gear's ordination was made the beginning of another protracted meeting, which was attended, like the last, with a visitation of the Spirit of grace. Ten

* Baptist Magazine, vol. xvi. p. 96. In the same place, record is made also of a female donation from Canton, of "old gold," — a sort of contribution then much in fashion.

were baptized by the pastor; and when he left the place, in December, the church numbered ninety-five. In the same month, a committee was authorized to request the Rev. James M. Coley to preach here for "the ensuing winter." Brother Coley remained with the church till March, and devoted himself faithfully to its interests.

By this time the meeting-house had become too strait to hold the congregation; and, during his stay, Brother Coley, with two others, was charged with the circulation of the first subscription-paper, the object being "to enlarge the old meeting-house, or build a new one." (86) But little was accomplished, however, in raising money, at this early day; and no alterations were attempted in the old meeting-house, the church being generally dissatisfied with the location, and deeming it better to build anew so soon as the proper time for it should come. A beginning only was made; and they who labored at that time for the present house contented themselves to wait, or, like David to Solomon, transmitted their gatherings to their successors. This winter, Brother Coley baptized five. The church-letter testifies that more additions were received in 1832 than in any previous year, but at the same time states that the church was "not so lively as was desirable." A disposition to do something for the cause of Christ abroad was apparent, however, chiefly among the sisters. It was probably during this winter or the following spring that a few of them pledged themselves to make up the sum of twenty-five dollars a year to pay for educating a Burman girl under the name of Lucinda Gill. This contribution was continued several years.* It appears that at the time the first remittance arrived in Burmah (July, 1834) no Burman girl could be obtained to stay at the mission longer than six months. The first comer, after the arrival of the first instalment of the money, was named Lucinda Gill, and taught to read; and the remainder of the money probably went to the teaching of others to read.†

* Baptist Magazine, vol. xvii. 168.

† Letter of Mrs. H. M. Mason to Nabby Gill, July 14, 1834.

In 1833, Rev. David Pease* preached here during the months of February and March (perhaps longer, (86,88)); and measures were taken to secure his services as pastor. He declined a settlement, however; and in July the church had their attention called to a young brother named Carpenter,† who was studying for the ministry, at Newton. Brn. Charles Johnson and Joseph Hodges, jun., then also students at the same seminary, were appointed a committee to request Bro. Carpenter to visit Canton (by leave of Professor Knowles), and supply the pulpit. Bro. Carpenter preached here two Sabbaths; but nothing permanent resulted in the way of a settlement, the young licentiate being distrustful of his own abilities: and, in the following month, Bro. Henry Marchant was sent for, to preach, "with the idea of becoming our pastor." Bro. Marchant's ministrations were generally acceptable; but, for some reason, he was not retained.

The church reported itself to the Association of 1833, "at peace, and, on the whole, prosperous;" but there does not seem to have been a condition of things favorable to a stated ministry. Tradition reports, and the historian's judgment can infer, some of the secrets of that chronic misfortune of this church, its transitory pastorates. A too great partiality for *special measures* seems to have characterized it from the first. This feeling, fostered long, and encouraged by gratification from time to time, created, of course, an undue esteem for preachers *whose gifts* could produce an immediate revival; and the constant demand for and the transient and varying labors of such men unfitted the people to appreciate any other. Habituated to frequent changes, they saw little calamity in a pastoral separation, and took little care to prevent it. The hastily expressed opinion of a single member has repeatedly been sufficient to send a good man away: and, in consequence, the fleeting and rapidly successive pastorates which this church has witnessed since its record began appear like little

* Since of Sunderland.

† Since Rev. Mark Carpenter, of Brattleboro,' Vt., and father of the missionary, Rev. C. H. Carpenter, Professor in the Seminary at Rangoon.

"clouds without water," that chase one another year after year over the field, until the aggregated number of all the preachers who have brought the word of life to this people would surpass some of their own Sunday congregations* Surely no ecclesiastical body could expect to reap the full benefit or realize the objects of its incorporation, or gain proper depth of root as a growth of influential good in the community, so long as it would content itself with such a locomotive ministry. It is to be hoped that the sad lessons of later years have taught this church a more steady reliance upon the stated means of grace, and to regard a relationship of pastor and people that shall be *permanent*, when once divinely sanctioned, as one surety of a solid prosperity. May we continue to learn! May we learn well, and build together, long and strong and deep, like the architects of old Jerusalem, "with three rows of great stones and a row of new timber"!

Failing to secure an ordained minister, the church again resorted to the seminary for a supply; and, in August or September, Bro. Cornelius A. Thomas † was sent. (89) He pleased the people well. Part of his autumn vacation was spent here; and, in company with his friend Hodges, he represented the church at the Association; but he was unable to supply it while pursuing his studies, and Elder Marchant was again invited to tarry a while here. He staid until the 1st of April, 1834, receiving seven dollars a week for his labors; and after him came again the young student Thomas, who staid over one or two Sabbaths, making up in both visits a stay of six weeks with the church.

An interval of a year or more followed, during which little or no effort seems to have been made to obtain a pastor; and the church was supplied with preaching from Newton and elsewhere. As if in anticipation of this, they had voted that "*in future*" the remuneration for pulpit-services should be five dollars

* It is remarkable that this church has had, during its fifty years, the same number of pastors as the First Baptist Church in Boston, now two hundred years old.

† Now Dr. Thomas, of Brandon, Vt., — "A very able, substantial, and revered minister of the gospel." — *Dr. Ripley.*

a Sabbath. In this interval, a younger brother of Dr. Hague, John B. Hague, a name not unfamiliar among the devotional poets of the Psalmist Hymn-book,* spent some time here during the long vacation at the Newton seminary, and prepared the letter and represented the church as delegate to the Association, in September, 1834. The people liked his preaching; and many to this day mention with pleasure his stay here, and tell of his social, musical, and pulpit gifts. After him, in the following spring, Bro. Darius Dunbar,† also a student at Newton, supplied here for a time, and was a member of the church until the 29th of April. (93)

Meanwhile the church-roll kept steadily diminishing, chiefly, however, by dismissions; until from ninety-eight (or, according to the Minutes, one hundred and three), in 1833, the list fell, by September, 1835, to seventy-five. During this year, two died, and four were excluded; and the church-letter reported "some trials and discouragements."

On the 28th of September, the subject of a new meeting-house was again brought before the church, and this time with a full purpose to build immediately. A committee was appointed to buy ground "at the village in the south-west part of the town;" and a vote was passed to sell the old meeting-house to the best advantage, and appropriate the proceeds to the new building.‡ The re-action of "trials and discouragements" is oftentimes the activity that saves a church. Here a step so important as the erection of a new house of worship was ventured upon in a time of weakness; but God helped the people.

A piece of land was bought of Mr. Gerry Tucker, in the south village, opposite the Armory Hall, at a cost of two hundred and thirty dollars; and there, in due time, the corner-stone of the present meeting-house was laid. Bro. James F. Wilcox, then a recent graduate of Newton Theological

* See Hymn 454, "Hark, sinner, while God from on high," &c.

† Now of Titicut.

‡ The meeting at which this action was taken was opened with prayer by Father William Bentley, of Hartford, Conn.

Seminary,* was spending the autumn here,[(97)] and entered into the enterprise with his whole soul. Besides supplying the pulpit, he aided the church by advising with them and raising money for them. They called him to the pastorate;[(99)] and, though he ultimately declined settling here, he remained with the people long enough to forward their new work through a good beginning, and to see it prospering in their hands.

During the same season (Nov. 21, 1835), the Ladies' Benevolent Society connected with this church was organized, and began to render systematic aid in the charities of the church, and in the general support of the means of grace. Like the church itself, it has had a varying history; but, as an auxiliary society, it has been an undoubted blessing to the cause. Only two of its first officers are still with us.

Rev. Asaph Merriam was settled here in the ministry in September of the year 1836, when the new meeting-house was still in progress. The old house ceased to be the property of the parish in the following January, being deeded to the town at about that date for six hundred and fifty dollars; † but he officiated there until the completion of the present house in June.

The church now rejoiced in a more commodious place of worship. The building stood as it now stands, (see frontispiece) fifty-six feet long by forty-one feet wide (exclusive of the present pulpit projection); being made, by the advice of Bro. Wilcox, a foot longer and a foot narrower than the original plan. The external appearance has not changed, with the exception of an enlargement at the north end to make the recess for the present pulpit; but the internal arrangements, as they were left by the finishers twenty-seven years ago, have entirely disappeared. Then the pews were high, upright enclosures, with a raised floor, considerably above the level of the aisles; the gallery, then two feet higher than now, had a straight front

* Laboring since 1861, for the Home-Mission Society, at Northfield, Minn.

† See Town Records, 1836-7; Church Records, p. 101.

from wall to wall; a large stove stood midway between the doors; and directly opposite, at the other end, just over the spot where the communion-table now stands, the pulpit, with its two swing-doors and winding staircases with banisters, rose against the north wall, then flush from east to west, and reached, with its top wood-work, nearly as high as the present side-lights. The cost of the building was about three thousand three hundred dollars.

The services of the dedication took place on the 13th of June, 1837; a crowded congregation being in attendance. Rev. Baron Stow, now Dr. Stow, of Chauncey-street Church, Boston, preached the sermon, from Heb. xi. 16: "But now they desire a better country; that is, a heavenly: wherefore God is not ashamed to be called their God; for he hath prepared for them a city." Pastor Merriam offered the dedicatory prayer; the choir furnished appropriate music; and the concluding prayer was offered by Rev. Mr. Sawyer, of Randolph. (104)

Shortly after, a courteous application was made to Mr. Benjamin Bussey, of Roxbury, for a bell. He had been formerly a resident of Canton, and, being wealthy, was in the habit of presenting church-bells to religious societies of his acquaintance that had just completed houses of worship. On this occasion, however, the committee which waited on him did not find him sufficiently indifferent to denominational distinctions to make his customary donation. Baptists did not come under the conditions of his generosity. The bell, therefore, was purchased of the Revere Copper Company, at a cost of a little more than two hundred and fifty dollars, and hung in 1839. Harrison Carroll was the first sexton.

The prospects of the church, at this time, were outwardly encouraging. Mr. Merriam's preaching was thronged from Sabbath to Sabbath; and the pews sold for nearly if not quite a sufficient sum to support him comfortably, and defray the current expenses of the year: * but the *internal* life of the

* It should be mentioned that the Congregationalist society was accustomed to worship with this church after the building of the present meeting-house, they having

church was far from what could have been wished. This fact was felt and acknowledged, and the yearly letter for 1838 makes regretful mention of spiritual apathy and coldness. A committee had been chosen in May, previous to the dedication of the meeting-house, "to visit every member of the church,"(103) and hold personal conversation with all concerning their spiritual state, entreating the delinquent and warning the refractory. Many sad cases of discipline were forced upon Bro. Merriam, and several were excluded during his stay. It sorely pained him, one of the most tender-hearted of men, to exclude a member from the church; and it is common to find at the close of the notices of such action in the records (which were then kept by himself) an observation like this: "The health and even life of the body sometimes requires the cutting off of a diseased limb. . . . May God convince the delinquents of their error, and bring them back to the fold of the Saviour!"

At the close of the associational year, September, 1839, the church numbered but sixty-two. Mr. Merriam resigned its charge, and removed to Athol. In the language of one who has gone over this record of years before me, "In our new house, we were not satisfied with our old minister."* I am not to decide here whether that dissatisfaction was fortunate. Events that followed were, and will continue to be, differently accounted for; and even the wise would differ as to what they proved.

Asaph Merriam was born in Gardner, Mass., March 20, 1792. He made a profession of religion in 1817, and was licensed to preach in 1824. His education for the ministry was chiefly acquired at the academy in New Ipswich, N.H., and under private instructors. He received ordination in the fall of 1825, at the meeting of the Wendell (now Miller's River) Association, in Royalston, Mass., as pastor jointly of the Bap-

at that day no stated services in their own house; also that there was then no Universalist society: so that the Baptist meeting was substantially the only one in the village.

* Hist. Canton Bap. Church, published in Min. Boston So. Assoc. 1850.

Asaph Merriam.

tist churches of Royalston and Warwick. He has since spent forty years in ministerial labor, and now resides in South Lyndeboro', N.H., an old man waiting for the summons of his Master.*

In May, previous to the resignation of Bro. Merriam, the church had invited Elder William Miller, the afterwards renowned herald of the Second Advent, then a humble Baptist preacher, to lecture in this place on the prophecies. The people seemed to crave some stimulating doctrine; and, hearing of his meetings in Randolph and Stoughton, they requested the pastor to invite him by letter to preach in this meeting-house. He consented; but it was not till several months afterwards that he came.

The same meeting that voted to dismiss Brother Merriam voted also to extend a call to the Rev. CHARLES O. KIMBALL, of Methuen, to come and settle in his room. He accepted the call, and shortly after moved here, and began to preach. The people soon became attached to him; for he was energetic, gifted, and pleasing, and his prospects of usefulness in this field were fair. But alas for the frailty of all human confidences! After preaching a little more than six weeks, the new pastor was, to the great surprise and grief of the church, convicted of conduct unworthy of his office, and deposed by council.(103)†

Charles Otis Kimball was twenty-three years in the ministry. He was born in Bradford, Mass., Sept. 25, 1791, and baptized in Haverhill, of this State, by Rev. William Batchelder, April 4, 1813, with whom, after an academical course in his native town, he studied for the ministry. He received his license of the First Baptist Church, in Haverhill, Aug. 19, 1814.‡ Two years afterwards (May 8, 1816), he was ordained in Methuen, where he labored long with great favor and usefulness. After the misfortune which cut him off from the ministry, he made his home in Canton, with his family,

* Preached in Canton, Oct. 30, 1864, and spent five days.

† Held in Boston, Nov. 20, 1839.

‡ Two months after the constitution of this church, the last one he ever served.

until the spring of 1843; enjoying for the latter portion of that time, by recommendation from Charlestown, the fellowship of this church. The Canton Sabbath-school Teachers' Association, formed here April 8, 1841, owed its organization to his zeal and Christian enterprise. He died in hope, July 24, 1854, at West Charleston, Vt. No picture of him remains. He was a man of medium stature, strongly built, with a countenance made prepossessing by sparkling dark eyes and great vivacity of expression. In the pulpit his utterance was rapid, and his manner there and elsewhere interesting and earnest.

Charles O Kimball

While the people were chafing under the frustration of their hopes in their late pastor, the contemplated visit of Elder Miller was made; and indeed it seemed to be providentially ordered, on purpose to divert their minds from their sudden affliction. Coming thus fortunately, his discourses, so far from producing here the mischiefs attendant on the preaching elsewhere of the doctrine contained in them, seem to have left, on the whole, a salutary impression; and there are Christian hearts now with us that date one great awakening of their spiritual life to the time when Elder Miller preached in this house the second coming of the Saviour.

Recovering from the shock of their disappointment in the case of Mr. Kimball, the people, in January of the following year, gave an invitation to Rev. HENRY CLARK, of Taunton, to assume the pastorate. He had already supplied the pulpit some time; and, finding the minds of the congregation serious from the recent addresses of Mr. Miller, he had the more easily affected their hearts by his presentation of truth. A deep religious interest had been awakened; and in the spring he removed to Canton in response to the call, the church agreeing to pay him the (for them unusual) salary of seven hundred dollars a year.

Pastor and people now labored together with wonderful success. Converts multiplied, both men and women, and of all ages, from the stripling to the man of gray hairs. Every month, from December, 1839, to August, 1840, inclusive, new accessions by baptism swelled the ranks of the church. Despondent ones gathered hope as they looked on; and veteran Christians, who had waited by the ark of God through evil days, thanked him that their prayers were answered.

In the language of the letter to the Association, "The work, for stillness and order and power, was peculiarly interesting; . . . in all respects, a greater work than was ever before known in our town." (119) The number of church-members reported for that year was one hundred and twenty-three; the Minutes giving an addition of fifty-one.

On the 10th of November, 1840, the church voted to invest their ministerial fund in real estate. The immediate cause of this action was their desire to build a *parsonage.* For a long time it had been difficult to find a dwelling-place for the minister; and, as the difficulty was growing greater, the demand for a house of their own forced itself upon the church more and more strongly. Money was necessary for this object; and at last it was resolved to make use of the two-thousand-dollar fund.

A spot of land was selected in the parish yard, on the *west* side of the meeting-house, and proposals were made to purchase of Thomas Tolman, Esq., an additional quarter of an acre on which to build a barn. On consideration, however, it was thought best to abandon that location; and the ground for the parsonage was staked out on the *east* side of the meeting-house, where it now stands, twenty-five feet more being purchased off Ezra Tilden's land to complete the requisite dimensions. The building-committee were instructed to proceed with the house at once, and the parsonage was completed before the winter of 1841, at a cost of one thousand six hundred and twenty-five dollars. (189, 90) The remainder of the fund (three hundred and seventy-five dollars) was loaned to the treasurer of the church, and, along with money raised by special subscription, was applied to paying off a mortgage of eight hundred dollars, which remained on the meeting-house. The barn, or "stable," stood in the yard a little north of the dwelling-house, until 1848, when it was removed to make room for the chapel.

This year also (1841), the sheds (all or some of them) were put up at the back of the meeting-house by private individuals under permission from the church.

Deacon Jason Houghton, after serving as first deacon of the church for almost a quarter of a century, had resigned his office on the 7th of April, 1839, and removed from the place. Deacon Crane had never consented to the appointment given him eight years before (p. 46) and never wrote himself deacon, nor is he ever so called by Mr. Merriam in the records. Being obliged to officiate much, however, as deacon, the younger portion of the church became accustomed to address him as "Deacon Crane;" and both Clerks Tucker and Capen write him as such. Whether nominal or real, he had been the only deacon for nearly two years; and the church were called upon now to supply two officers to that station by regular election. They met on the 9th of December, 1840, and, after prayer and due deliberation, made choice of Ezekiel Capen and George Lothrop.

The 22d of August, 1841, was set apart by the church as a special fast. After this, frequent meetings were held, additions were received from time to time up to the forepart of the following summer, until, at the closing-up of Bro. Clark's ministry here, the number of members in this fellowship had reached its maximum, — one hundred and forty-four. During his pastorate, Brother Clark baptized sixty-two. His resignation was accepted by the church on the 19th of June, 1842; a strong effort having been previously made to retain him.

Henry Clark was born in Canterbury, Conn., Nov. 12, 1810. He was converted to God in the autumn of 1829, licensed to preach in 1832, and pursued his preparatory studies in Madison University. In June, 1834, he was ordained over the Baptist Church in Seekonk, where he continued to labor, with

Henry Clark

the exception of a little more than two years, in Taunton, until his settlement with this church. He resides at present in Pittsfield, having been unable to preach for several years in consequence of a loss of voice.*

It now becomes the sad duty of the faithful historian to record a long decline. It may be said, and doubtless with truth, that this was partly owing to re-action, and partly to removals; but though these may account for the numerical depletion, and some falling off of zeal, a deeper reason must be sought for the spiritual relapse from which it took more than eight years to recover. That the elements of decline existed under the very prosperity of the foregoing years is no unexampled fact. Unsafe and insufficient sources of joy generally escape exposure till the rapture and the glow are gone. The time for careful discrimination was before the revival begun, when the church was being disciplined by misfortune and disappointment. Afterwards, when the warnings and exhortations of Christians were heard in the excitement of success, they often seemed harsh, and were too likely to be so. The experience of centuries shows that periods of religious power and conquest are almost always attended by excesses in religious people; and the revival now in question was no exception to the rule.† The consequences of these were doubtless experienced in the season of desolation which followed.

By every law of Providence and of grace, a blessing should have followed the system (or a similar one) of parish-visiting begun in the pastorate of Elder Merriam, had it been patiently pursued. A work of reformation springing up quietly in the

* Visited Canton and preached, Sept. 3, 1865.

† It is remarkable that Whitefield's preaching, and the religious movement attending it, were followed, more or less, by the sad fruits of imprudent zeal in dealing with the ungodly. Dr. Baron Stow, speaking of the spirit of bitterness which was roused in many quarters against that remarkable man, says, "Much of the hostility was provoked by improprieties of both speech and action, that would at any time be offensive to those who love good order and Christian decorum." Certainly we are not to blame the ungodly less for rejecting the truth; but we should charge ourselves the more to avoid needlessly exasperating them when we present it to them." — *Belcher's Whitefield*, p. 92.

bosom of the church must ever be the fruit of seed sown in prayer and preaching and social faithfulness; and such a reformation could never have left the church dependent for its future prosperity on mere numbers or on particular men. There were many things to be thankful for in the great revival of 1840, and its results; and, though not seen to be such at the time, the "dark age" that followed it was one of them. A sounder and safer piety came out of that long trial. God always turns to the best good of his people the misfortunes which, but for their want of wisdom, would more seldom be.

September, 1842, came, and the Canton Church reported itself to the Association, one hundred and forty-three members, and a Sunday school of one hundred pupils in fourteen classes, and a large Bible class; but it was pastorless, and there is a touch of sadness in the letter, where it says, "Last spring we anticipated a glorious revival, but were doomed to be disappointed." Many of those who then looked for a descent of the Holy Spirit were far away — some asleep in the church-yard — before that blessing came again to Canton.

Meanwhile, the "contradiction of sinners" exhibited itself in the usual ways. From the beginning of the year 1840, or near the very commencement of the revival in the Baptist meetings, the enemies of evangelical religion wrought with unwonted diligence against the cause. Many, offended at the pungent preaching of Mr. Clark, left the congregation entirely.

The elements of opposition soon became organized, and assumed a sectarian character; and a new church, with a freer latitude of faith, was the result. The novelty of their enterprise, and the congeniality of their creed, drew many to the meetings of these people; and it began to be evident that the Baptists must divide their ancient congregation with others. It soon became no less evident, that the apostasy had entered the pale of the communion. A few back-slidden and discontented ones, who had long shrunk from facing the humbling truths and fearful rebukes of the New Testament, were willing to abandon a church which enforced them, and embrace the accommodating doctrines of liberal religion.(140) Expulsions began early in 1841;(124) and, from that time, cases of discipline multiplied. The severity shown and felt to be necessary in some of these imbittered the incipient prejudices of many, and alienated the already wavering attachment of individuals, and even families. At the same time, removals weakened the numerical strength of the church. The burning of the large Bolivar Factory, in 1841, threw nearly twenty of the members out of employment, and obliged them, soon after, to seek other homes. The remainder became disheartened. They found their resources diminishing, and their burdens increasing; and leaning, as they had unconsciously learned to do, upon the arm of flesh, it was with a faint and feeble animation that they continued to support the stated means of grace. For a part of the time they were supplied with preaching from Newton; and Rev. Joseph W. Eaton* performed the duties of a pastor here a while in 1842 and 1843.

In June, 1843, Rev. Lewis Holmes accepted a call, and labored here about two years; but neither the church funds nor the church spirit were up to the standard of a stated ministry. The roll of membership also was lessening by dismissions at the rate of two per month; and Bro. Holmes was obliged to remove in the spring of 1845, for lack of support.(142) We must suppose, that, under these circumstances of the church, the contributions for benevolent purposes could not be large. In fact, they fell off entirely at last, with the exception of an occasional remittance by individuals, and an annuity from the Female Mite Society, organized in November, 1843, which educated a Burman girl under the name of Abby Crane, and continued till 1851 to remit seventeen dollars a year.†

Among the many who removed from the town during this season of discouragement was Dea. George Lothrop, who was dismissed to Newark, N.J., on the 24th of September, 1843, while Bro. Holmes was pastor. The church was thus left again with a single deacon. For three years,

* Now of Cambridgeport.

† Rec. Ladies' Benev. Soc., vol. i. p. 29.; Bap. Mag. 1842.

Dea. Capen served the church unassisted;* till on the 2d of October, 1846, Bro. Willard Shepard was chosen junior deacon, and still retains the office.

Lewis Holmes was born in Plymouth, Mass., April 12, 1813; baptized by Rev. Thomas Conant in June, 1831; and graduated from Waterville College in 1840. He was ordained at Edgartown, Marth. Vin., June 10, 1841. His present place of labor is North Scituate.

In May, 1845, Rev. TIMOTHY C. TINGLEY was invited to the pastorate here; and in the following month, with his wife and sister, joined the church. During the period of his ministry, the movement to build a new chapel was agitating the minds of the church. Deacon Crane died March 27, 1847, and left, among other bequests, the sum of seven hundred dollars to build a chapel in the parish grounds "on the east side of the meeting-house, near the north line." Difficulties arose unforeseen by the lamented donor, which complicated the matter, and delayed the benefits of the bequest a long time; but at length, during the year 1850, the present neat and convenient building was erected, and has ever since been the place of meeting for weekly lectures, and conferences of the church.

The vestry underneath the meeting-house was damp and unwholesome; and Deacon Crane himself had, with others, experienced the ill effects of long sittings there. Besides, a school had been kept in it for a while,[127, 143, 169] and the children had disfigured the room; and the practice of renting it to occasional lecturers had somewhat impaired the sacredness of the place, and left it the worse for wear and tear. The new chapel was needed, and proved (as may it long prove!) a most welcome gift.

It was during this period, also, that the connection of this church with the Boston Association was dissolved. In September, 1847, it petitioned to be set off, to help form a new

* This faithful officer, like Deacon Crane and his early co-laborers, eminently deserves the title of Friend of the Church. Since his connection here in 1839, his person and his purse have ever been at its service. In some of its feeblest days, he has supported almost alone its pulpit supplies and stated contributions, and been its deacon, sexton, Sabbath-school superintendent, treasurer, and clerk.

Sam Holmes

J. C. Tingley,

body under the name of the "Norfolk Baptist Association;" but, in February of the following year, the old Boston Association was divided, and Canton was embraced in the Boston South, where it still remains.

A note of a little more than two hundred and fifty dollars held at the bank here, and another of two hundred and thirteen dollars held by a private individual against the church, were paid during Bro. Tingley's ministry, and the parsonage was repaired: but the pastor's salary, instead of being increased, was diminished;* and, after a term of three years and a half, he resigned his place. He removed from Canton in November, 1848.(167)

Timothy Cheever Tingley was born in Cumberland, R.I., July 4, 1804, and studied at Brown University. He was licensed in North Attleboro', October, 1828; graduated from Newton Theological Seminary † in 1831; and ordained at Foxboro' on the 14th of July of the same year. He is now preaching at Somerset. During his pastorate here, according to the records, nineteen were dismissed, ten were expelled, three were dropped, one died, and nine were added by letter.

In the fall of 1848, ‡ Rev. John W. Olmsted, now Dr. Olmsted of the "Watchman and Reflector," was secured as a stated supply, and continued to preach here with much acceptance for more than two years (to April, 1851).

Matters had now apparently come to a crisis in the history of the church's decline. The church list was reduced to seventy. With eight years of famine in the past, uncheered by one baptismal season or one conversion, the church now waited and prayed. For a time the importunate calls of discipline subsided, and brethren and sisters had time to wonder and search their own hearts.

* Treasurer's Book, pp. 57, 58 (1847), with pp. 60, 61 (1848).

† He was class-mate and room-mate in the Seminary with Hiram Gear, the fifth pastor.

‡ It was towards the close of the year 1848 that the addition of eleven feet was built on to the rear of the parsonage, rendering the house much more comfortable and convenient; and in the following spring the parsonage was newly painted.

What could it mean? For twice four years, faithful preachers of Christ, men of blameless lives and pure zeal, had proclaimed the truth among them, and not the first sheaf of a spiritual harvest had been gathered! An impostor, an alien in the fold of God, had, nineteen years before, preached in the same community, and stirred the people, and reaped wonderful results in single evenings! But, as for these good men, they met with no response. Season after season, the ambassadors of Christ in this pulpit had been like children sitting in the market-place, and calling unto their fellows, "We have piped unto you, and ye have not danced; we have mourned unto you, and ye have not lamented." Why were they not permitted to build up the church?* The materials lay all around them. Oh for the power of the fabled magician, whose voice and harp could charm the scattered stones into a stately tower! But no: they must wait till God had perfected the patience of his saints, and then his breath would wake the sleeping and revive the slain. Never had this people been so thoroughly convinced of the total inefficiency of human power; never had seen so clearly the utter foolishness of preaching, and the sovereignty of Him who can let his enemies prosper, and the suffering cause of his own chosen pass over unheard till the great day.

They were humbled, and the way was prepared for the coming of the Comforter.

Before Bro. Olmsted closed his labors here, the condition of the church was, upon the whole, improving. More in-

* A tradition prevailed among the older members of the church (p. 4), that, when Whitefield was refused the liberty of preaching here in 1740, he prophesied that there would be no visitation of the Holy Ghost to the place till that generation passed away. This saying has been echoed by recent ministers, as if it purported a *perpetual* curse of spiritual barrenness; an error which is soon corrected by reflection, and contradicted by subsequent facts. If Whitefield ever uttered such a prediction of the town (and in the only account which bears any resemblance to the tradition, see Belcher's Whitefield, p. 195, a village is specified which is "now a city," and could not, therefore, be Canton), the generation which passed away in the last century fulfilled it in the church which denied him a hearing. The Baptists certainly deserve no share in the curses of Whitefield, since, so far from rejecting his ministrations, they everywhere grew and multiplied under them, and rejoiced to rank themselves with the great body of proscribed New Lights whom his preaching drew away from the standing order.

terest in religion was manifested; and there seemed to be a general readiness to welcome a settled pastor, and co-operate with him in labors to advance the interests of the kingdom of Christ.

In April, 1851, Bro. DAVID B. FORD, of Scituate, an alumnus of the Newton Seminary, who had preached several times in Canton, was invited to spend a week among the people. The visit was made, and to so much mutual satisfaction, that he staid until July, when he received and accepted a unanimous call to settle here as pastor.

Meanwhile, the church, having had the subject under consideration since early in 1849, in hope of aid and benefit from the union, joined with itself a society. The organization took place on the 8th of June, 1851.*

The cause of religion now began slowly to revive. One prominent member, who had previously fallen into sceptical views and been excluded, was, upon confession, in the same meeting which called Bro. Ford, restored to the communion. Another excluded member was restored the following April.(182)

Eighteen hundred and fifty-one was the world's year of peace. The nations had forgotten for a while their feuds, and employed the universal respite from bloodshed in assembling industrial congresses, and forwarding the healthful enterprises of science and religion. Many a faltering good cause found its opportunity in that silent jubilee, when the dial-hands of the nineteenth century, still pointing to noon, seemed to wait for God's people to invoke a future of better things; and peradventure this little church partook the general benediction of the year, and began from thence the ascending way to a surer prosperity. Such a hope now dwelt, though feebly, in the bosoms of the members; and an outline of the church's history, published in the Minutes for 1850, closes with some words of encouragement. The church and pastor labored

* After this date, many matters of interest, formerly recorded in the church-book, will be found in the society-records.

together harmoniously, and ere long their hearts were cheered by the conversion of souls.

Bro. Ford was ordained here on the 25th of September, 1851; Rev. Isaac Smith, now of Foxboro', preaching the sermon; and Rev. George W. Sampson, now Dr. Sampson, of Washington, presenting the right hand of fellowship. Rev. Jeremiah Chaplin, since of Newton, gave the charge to the candidate; and Rev. Silas Ripley offered the ordaining prayer. Other parts in the service were borne by Revs. Thomas Driver, J. W. Olmsted, Alfred Colburn, and George Tucker. Sharon, Foxboro', West and East Dedham, Jamaica Plain, Randolph, and East Stoughton, supplied the ordaining council.

In March, 1852, the minds of so large a number in the church became exercised in favor of open communion, that the following resolution was drafted and presented: —

"Regarding a compliance of our Saviour's command, to 'believe and be baptized,' requisite for admission to his table, we see no just reason why all such persons as have a good standing in any evangelical church, in obedience to such requisition of our Lord, should not be admitted to his table, to celebrate with us the gospel ordinance of the Lord's Supper. Therefore

Resolved, That this church, hereafter, give the following invitation at their communion service: *'All baptized believers in good standing in any evangelical church are invited to a seat with us at the Lord's table.'*" (181)

This resolution was adopted "unanimously;" (182) but the majority, finding afterwards that a minority (probably not present at its adoption) were dissatisfied with this change, after a kind and temperate discussion at the next monthly meeting, consented to a reconsideration, and the matter was left where it had been before the vote.(183) Any future member, curious to know how well this church deserves a "liberal" reputation, can have to think that it was avowedly an open-communion church just twenty-eight days and twenty-eight nights.

In the months of March and April, twelve were baptized; and before May, 1853, eight more. Bro. Ford's pastorate was in the main a pleasant one, though, like that of all his predecessors, brief. His name will ever be connected in the

David B. Ford

memory of the church with her sixth revival. A few cases of discipline became necessary during his stay here, and one was excluded as unworthy; but the church had received strength again, and was able to hold her own. The ladies of the society enlisted with special energy, replenished the baptismal wardrobe, and improved the interior of the meeting-house at an expense of nearly seventy dollars.*

Failing health obliged Bro. Ford to resign towards the close of his third year; and in November, 1853, he was dismissed from his charge.

David Barnes Ford was born in South Scituate, Nov. 10, 1820; fitted for college in Hanover Academy, in that place; and graduated at Brown University in 1845. He studied theology at Newton, and was Hebrew tutor there after his graduation in 1848. He now resides in South Scituate, and supplies the pulpit of the First Baptist Church in Marshfield. Since leaving this place, he has published several articles in the "Biblotheca Sacra," "Christian Review," and "Boston Review," and translated, jointly with Professor Hovey, Perthe's "Life and Times of John Chrysostom."

Rev. PHILEMON R. RUSSELL was the next pastor. He was settled here in April, 1854; having previously supplied the pulpit for several weeks. He found the church numbering ninety-six members, and labored among them three years, going much from house to house, and exhorting them to fidelity and good works.

It was during his pastorate that the society procured the organ which now stands in the choir.† This was purchased in the spring of 1855, chiefly through the enterprise of the ladies, who persuaded the society to obtain it, and raised the necessary funds by subscription. Mr. E. L. Holbrook, of East Medway, was the builder.

Philemon Robbins Russell was born in Bath, Me., March 10, 1807; was hopefully converted in 1826, and, after prepar-

* Rec. Ladies' Benevolent Soc., vol. ii. pp. 7, 10.

† In that time, also, the fence was built in front of the meeting-house (1855).

ing for the ministry under private tuition in his native town, he was ordained in Winchester, N.H., in 1831. According to the records, he received five into the church by baptism during his ministry in Canton. He now resides in Lynn.*

After remaining destitute of a pastor about six months, during which time Bro. George Howell † preached here several times as a candidate, the church called and settled Rev. GEORGE W. HERVEY. He supplied them ably with the ministry of the word, from early in January, 1858, to the 1st of July, 1861, baptizing in that time sixteen. While he preached here, the church sent out one young minister, Rev. Oliver P. Fuller, now of Centreville, R.I. He was not licensed here, having been connected with another church during his studies in Middleboro' and Providence; but his home was here, and the brethren and sisters here from time to time gave him aid and encouragement. The 11th of February, 1859, was made the pleasant occasion of a presentation to this young brother of a purse of sixty dollars by Mr. Hervey, on behalf of the church and society, and of a handsome watch by the ladies.‡ It was also during Bro. Hervey's pastorate that the church purchased its new communion-service.

George Winifred Hervey was born in South Durham, N.Y., Nov. 28, 1821. Converted while studying law, he turned his attention to the ministry, and was licensed to preach in 1842. He began his collegiate studies at Madison University, and was graduated from Columbia College, Washington, in 1847, subsequently receiving the master's degree from the University of Rochester. He was ordained in April, 1850, by the Amity-street Baptist Church, in New York City, and settled successively at Upper Middletown, Conn., and Hudson, N.Y., prior to his pastorate in Canton. He spent the year 1856 in European study and travel. He is the author of two works on practical ethics, the one entitled "The Principles of Courtesy," and the other, "The Rhetoric of Conversation," published by Messrs. Harper & Bros. The latter

* Visited Canton and preached, March 26, 1865.

† Since become an Episcopalian, and now preaching in Waltham.

‡ Rec. Ladies' Benevolent Soc., vol. ii. p. 43.

P. B. Russell

G. W. Hervey

work has been republished in London. He has also published a sermon preached by him in this place, Jan. 4, 1861, entitled "Liberty a Cloak of Maliciousness," and several articles in the "Christian Review;" one on "Congregational Singing," another on "Hereditary Depravity," translated from the German, and another entitled "Spurgeon as a Preacher." Bro. Hervey is at present doing the work of an evangelist in and near New-York City.

After an interval of three months, during which time different preachers occupied the pulpit, — Rev. W. H. Watson, of Natick, coming once to administer the ordinance of baptism, and Bro. Chapin H. Carpenter,* the missionary, supplying here once or twice from the seminary at Newton, — Bro. A. F. Mason † began to labor here in the ministry, and continued with the church until July, 1862, preaching and baptizing. The church signified their desire that he should remain with them a year from that date; but he declined, believing that the providence of God called him to another field. During his stay here, the church received an accession of six to its membership.

The question of altering and repairing the meeting-house was voted upon this year; and, after considerable discussion in church and society, it was determined to begin at once, and carry through the contemplated work before the times grew harder. Accordingly, in the spring of 1862, the repairs were commenced, and carried vigorously forward through the summer, until, on the first Sabbath in October, Bro. Samuel K. Dexter, a young student at Hamilton, who had preached to the people in the chapel during his vacation, held the first service in the remodelled church.

It proved fortunate that this work was accomplished so soon, as, otherwise, it might have been delayed till the house was too old to be repaired. The distress felt from the war to-day precludes the possibility of any extraordinary outlay for years to come.

* Son of Rev. Mark Carpenter (p. 49), and now in Rangoon.

† Since of New-York City.

Among other alterations, the old bell hung in 1839 was exchanged at this time for the cast-steel one which now hangs in the belfry.

In November of this year, Rev. A. W. Carr began to supply the pulpit; and, on the 9th of December, the church extended him a call. This call he ultimately declined, although at first he gave the people some encouragement to expect him; and in March, 1863, Rev. THERON BROWN, the present pastor, came here by unanimous invitation, having supplied the church most of the time since the middle of January.

Theron Brown was born in Willimantic, Conn., April 29, 1832. He indulged a hope in Christ in the winter of 1850–51, and turned his attention to the ministry. His preparatory studies were pursued at the Connecticut Literary Institution in Suffield; at Yale College, where he took his degree in 1856; at the Theological School on East Windsor Hill; and at Newton Theological Seminary, from which he was graduated in June, 1859. On the 15th of December in the same year, he was ordained over the Baptist Church in South Framingham, having preached more or less as a licentiate of the First Baptist Church in New Haven, Conn., since the fall of 1856. During the winter and spring of 1861–62, he spent another term of study at Newton, and subsequently, up to the commencement of his pastorate in Canton, was engaged chiefly in writing for religious journals.

I have purposely omitted to make any particular mention of the *sacred music* of the church, reserving what facts I found respecting that interesting department of its worship for a special notice at the end.

The ancient town of Stoughton, which included the present Canton, was the cradle of the New-England middle-age psalmody,— that strange, quaint, minor mode, with its "down-up" time and its complicated "fugues," whose most characteristic specimens are now preserved, and performed only as musical curiosities.

Theron Brown

"Portland," and "Sherburne," and "Bridgewater" and "Lenox," and "Windham" and "Lebanon," and "China" and "Majesty," and "New Jerusalem" and the "Easter Anthem," were all born upon this soil; and the familiar Canton names of Capen and Tilden and Tolman and French and Dickerman and Belcher appeared ninety years ago on the list of the singing-class of William Billings the composer, and were famous more or less in the old time, in the Stoughton Musical Society or Old Club.

The members of both the Canton choirs belonged, most of them, to the Old Club. It was an age of musical enthusiasm, when this church was young; and there were few in the town who could sing, that were not, or had not been, connected with the popular singing-school of Squire Dunbar, the "king of singers."* So familiar were the early members of this church with the old-fashioned music,† that no note-books were used in their meetings for seven years. Among them were several brethren and sisters, whom God had gifted in no mean degree with the talent of song. They loved the ancient, plaintive lays of Billings and Swan, and Holden and Reed, and Maxim and Edson and Belcher; and few ever sung them better than Friend Crane and Deacon Tilden. Upon them devolved the

* The *old* singers' list, to which reference has been made, bears date 1774, the year before the battle of Lexington. The Stoughton Musical Society was formed on the 7th of November, 1786. Samuel Tolman was the first leader. — *Histor. and Genealog. Reg.*, vol. xiv. pp. 252, 53.

† The following verses of Rev. Mather Byles (exactly rendered into the music of "Consonance, an Anthem") describe very well, even without the notes, the style of psalm-singing which prevailed largely in New-England church worship from the Revolution through the first quarter of the present century: —

"Down steers the BASS with grave majestic air,
And up the TREBLE mounts with shrill career:
With softer sounds, in mild, melodious maze,
Warbling between, the TENOR gently plays;
But if the inspiring ALTUS joins its force
See, like the lark, it wings its towering course.
From the bold height, it hails the echoing bass,
Which swells to meet and mix in close embrace.
Through different systems all the parts divide:
By music's chords, the distant notes are tied;
And sympathetic strains enchanting wind
Their restless race till all the parts are joined:
Then rolls the rapture through the air around
In the full, magic melody of sound."

duty of "starting the tune" in the days of the school-house meetings; and though the assembly was never so small, and even if no minister was present, there was sure to be no lack of song-worship provided *they* were there. Their children inherited much of their tunefulness, and many of the voices were youthful that sung when the gallery of the old meeting-house was first opened for divine praise.

The first notice of a choir appears immediately after the dedication of that meeting-house, when Oliver Hayden, a singing-master of Stoughton, receives an invitation to lead the singing.(27) Saving a tuning-fork and pitch-pipe, no instruments were used in that old-fashioned orchestra. The feelings of many of the congregation were against such artificial aids to worship; and indeed, when the whole force was mustered together, and the spirit of praise was fully on, there was little need of them. Wonders of melody were achieved when the four families of Belcher, Tucker, Tilden, and Crane, each a choir in itself, met, with all their combined strength and diversity of musical gifts, to sustain their several parts in one grand tune. Clifford Belcher * was the first chorister. He took the place at an early day (Hayden being only an occasional leader, and never residing in the place), and continued in it nearly twenty years. There was no disputing his claim to be leader. The splendid tenor of his voice rang above the rest like a trumpet. Clara Crane and her sisters Sarah and Julia, Caroline and Roxy Blackman, Ruth Houghton, Abigail Tilden, Ruth McKendry, and Caty Tucker, carried along the treble and counter-tenor like a chime; and the clear notes of Elisha Crane, and the leader's two sons Daniel and Clifford Belcher, most musically bore their part in the harmony. There too, Abner Tilden, and Samuel Tucker with his son Elias, and Ezra Tilden with his son Lemuel, came in in excellent time and tune; and the deep, rolling bass of Friend Crane, poured along underneath, and through and through the song, mixing itself with the melody, and still sounding as distinct as the

* Clifford Belcher was a nephew of *Supply* Belcher, author of one of the old music-books, and also of several pieces in the Stoughton Collection.

cornet stop of an organ. They who heard his wonderful voice will never forget it in life, and his surviving fellow-singers are never weary of talking about it. It is even said that his widow, by virtue of a sense peculiar to her own faith, hears at this day the grand tones of that now silent voice singing from beyond the grave the ancient anthems and psalms.

The first hymn-book of the Baptist choir was the original, *unexpurgated* edition of the "Psalms and Hymns" of Watts. Prior to this, an old collection, entitled "Hymns for the Use of Christians," had been in use in the meetings of the Baptists. This book has already been referred to (p. 5) as containing the hymns which expressed so appropriately the early situation and circumstances of the church. It was a queer miscellany, comprising some of the proudest and some of the poorest efforts of devotional rhyme. "My Soul's full of Glory," "Oh, when shall I see Jesus?" "Let Thy Kingdom, Blessed Saviour," "How Tedious and Tasteless the Hours!" "Come, all ye Christian Pilgrims," and the ancient favorite from the pen of Dr. Baldwin, "From whence doth this union arise?" are specimen hymns of this collection, familiar once to the proscribed Baptist worshippers as household words.

No note-books were in use before the meeting-house was built, such old tunes only being sung as dwelt in the people's memories: afterwards, for ten or twelve years, the choir sung out of the "Bridgewater Collection" and the "Village Choir." A vote of the church in July, 1832, authorizing the purchase of "six hymn-books and six singing-books for the use of the singing," refers probably to the latter book. At the time the old meeting-house was abandoned, they were singing from the "Washington Harmony." In May, 1837, it was voted to "purchase one dozen hymn-books and one dozen singing-books for the use of the choir." By this time, the singers had commenced the use of "Winchell's Watts;" and this is most likely the hymn-book referred to in the purchase.

As the younger generation came on, there began to be a demand for instrumental music. The movement to procure this was, at first, stoutly withstood by a few; but the many prevailed, and, before the church left the original house, a violincello was procured, and committed to the skilful hands of Capt. Elisha Crane, the son of Friend.*

Not long after the commencement of worship in the new house, a double-bass-viol was purchased; and, in the spring of 1841, the ladies presented the choir with a violin.† Elias Tucker played upon the first, and the smaller instrument was performed by Clifford Belcher, jun. By this time, the most strenuous opposers of instrumental music were dead; but there remained a few who felt their old repugnance revive at this reinforcement of stringed melody, and bestowed upon the new instruments the undignified designation of "fiddles."

Elias Tucker succeeded chorister Belcher in the duties and honors of the leadership. He came in at about the time of the great musical revival in the town. For a series of years, the singing had greatly deteriorated in the churches, till there seemed likely to be none, after the old natural voices were gone, to maintain the excellence of the ancient choirs.

Feeling deeply the desirableness of restoring an interest in sacred music, committees from all the religious societies met in 1840, and voted to request Mr. Lowell Mason to recommend to them a suitable teacher.

Mr. Mason recommended Horace Bird, who was at once engaged to come to this place and establish a singing-school. The effect was soon apparent in the improved quality of the singing in the Baptist and other churches. Mr. Bird's school was thronged. He labored here nearly two years, and completely revived the musical enthusiasm of the old time; and, at this day, he has the credit of making nearly all the old singers who are at present in the town. It is at least true, that he made a good part of the singers in the present Baptist choir.‡ Elias Tucker was one of his pupils. He was made leader in 1840, and has continued until now, through sunshine

* At first, this bass-viol was owned by Friend Crane; but in September, 1841, he presented it to the church. — Ch. Rec. p. 125.

† Rec. Ladies' Benevolent Soc., vol. i. p. 14.

‡ June, 1864. For the changes since then, see p. 76, note.

and through storm, faithful to the interests of the choir, until he has grown a veteran in the service. Andrew Lopez, the assistant chorister, also a pupil of Mr. Bird, has held his office for an equal term, and assisted the singing with distinguished ability.

After a time the double-bass-viol and violin grew tiresome, and were pronounced out of date. The violin was carried away, and its huge, three-stringed companion was condemned to stand silent in the corner of the gallery until the summer of 1849, when it was sold for the trifle of eighteen dollars and a half.

For five or six years prior to 1850 or thereabouts, the choir sung after the old fashion, having no instrumental music. Then the small seraphine,* now standing in the chapel, was carried in, and used more or less till the organ was set up.

Meanwhile, the tune-books had several times been changed. The "Boston Academy" succeeded the "Washington Harmony," and was in turn succeeded by the "Modern Psalmist." Then came the "Carmina Sacra," which holds its place yet as a sort of standard, always supplying a good tune when the lighter collections that lie on the gallery railing fail to furnish the leader with the proper music for the minister's hymn.

The interest felt by Deacon Crane in the choir continued unabated till his death, nor did his voice ever fail. Even during his last sickness, when he invited, as he loved to do, his fellow-singers into his room to sing him over the good old tunes, his round, rich bass would involuntarily break in, and continue, unshaken by his threescore years and ten, in perfect harmony to the close. One chief object in his provision for building a chapel was, as he told them when they stood around his bed, to secure *to the choir* a better place to meet and practice in.†

In the summer of 1851, the "Psalmist," our present church hymn-book, was procured, nor has the time quite come to supersede it. About the same time, Mr. E. W. Bray, a mem-

* Purchased by Deacon Capen.

† Deacon Crane died March 27, 1847, aged seventy. His last words were, "I want rest."

ber of the society, presented the church with a set of the "Cantica Laudis."

The twelve-stop organ now in the loft was built in 1855, by subscription, at a cost of about five hundred and fifty dollars. Miss Julia Crane, since Mrs. George Ames, a granddaughter of Friend Crane, who had played some time in the choir upon the old instrument, was the first organist. After her marriage, in 1856, the organ was played by Miss Eveline Knaggs, now Mrs. A. F. Mason. She continued until the end of the year 1862, when, on her removal from Canton, Miss Clara Lopez, daughter of the assistant chorister, took the organist's place, and still retains it.*

Besides the "Cantica Laudis," since the introduction of the "Carmina Sacra," the choir have used more or less the "Modern Harp," the "Bay-State Collection," the "Psaltery," and the "Harp of Judah."

For a chapel hymn-book, the "Christian Harp" was procured in 1856, and succeeded in 1861 by the "Sacred Lyre," which is still in use.

It is interesting to find two members of the choir of fifty years ago still represented in the singers' seats. Five of our present choir are descendants of Ezra Tilden and Samuel Tucker. May the new be in more respects than one the children of the old; and, when the time shall come for this choir and congregation to stand before the great white throne, may the voices of the first and last that sung or shall have sung the praises of God here, be lifted in eternal jubilee, where fifty years are but the twinkling of an eye, and a thousand years are as one day! †

It is a source of regret that I am not able to present any

* Until March, 1865.

† Since this history was written, the last descendant of the Tilden Family has left the choir, the two families of Mr. Lopez and Mr. J. Fisher having removed to Lawrence, Kan., on the 10th of March, 1865. The popular singing-school of Prof. H. L. Whitney, organized the same year in this village, has awakened an interest in sacred music fully equal to that in the days of Mr. Bird; and, under the new impulse, the choirs of the town are gradually re-organizing and improving.

accurate report of the church's *benevolence* during the period of its existence. Such a report could not fail to interest us; and had the successive clerks of this church realized how much the simple annual record of the church treasurer's reports, and statistics of occasional charities would have been worth to us now, they would in no case have omitted to make them.

As it is, these reports, with one or two unsatisfactory exceptions, were never engrossed on the church records until 1855; and so little pains has been taken to preserve the files, that only fragmentary copiës of the originals can be found — none of these reaching farther back than 1833. Many papers that would have thrown light upon this interesting article in our history have been carelessly or wilfully destroyed. In consequence of these combined fatalities, the memorial of the alms and home-charities of the church through forty years, to say nothing of the spontaneous contributions collected on the Sabbath now and then for a special cause or an occasional agent, has passed forever beyond recall. Perhaps it matters not if all that is given in faith have record in heaven; but we cannot help wishing that the good which our fathers did might be fairly told us while we are alive. Driven to gather what I could from the printed receipts of the Home and Foreign Missionary Magazines, I looked through twenty volumes of the former, and forty volumes of the latter, and wrote out the results of my search; but I cannot satisfy myself of their accuracy.

Much uncertainty, too, involves the stipendiary and business expenditures of the church, though less than in the other case. The first record of expenditure is five dollars for the sacramental elements in 1814. after which no financial data appear, from which a definite report can be made, until 1821. Deacon Tilden was appointed treasurer in 1818.(21) He had been appointed before in 1814, as related in the history of that year (p. 18); but there seems to have been little for a treasurer to do in the first three or four years, and his office became a sinecure. Indeed, for the whole time prior to 1821, the *incidental* expenses of the church must have been next to nothing, since they always held their meetings in private houses or at the North School-house, and could not have been at charges for a sexton, and very little, if any, for rent, lights, and fuel. As for preaching, the good brethren who supplied them at that early day generally expected nothing besides their expenses, which consisted chiefly in board and horse-keeping. Probably a hundred dollars a year would amply represent the current expenses of the church for the first five or six years, counting in every thing.

In 1818, moneys for the building of the meeting-house began to come in; and Deacon Tilden, being already Town treasurer, and a man of experience in such matters, was chosen to take the charge of them.* Through the two years that this house was in progress, the records are meagre; and nothing is known of its cost except by tradition.

The first definite notice of a vote to raise money for the support of preaching appears under date of January, 1821;(27) and from that date the yearly expenditures in this particular can be made out with tolerable certainty. In the Appendix will be given an estimate (as near as can be made) of the annual outlay of the church, based mainly on the records of the church and society, and on printed reports. The summing-up is as follows: —

Paid for preaching during the fifty years . . .	$18,591 00
Paid for building, repairing, and current expenses .	16,890 15
Paid for benevolent objects	3,528 04
Total	$39,009 19

Much praise is due to the ladies for the part they have borne in the charities of the church, and in the risks and burdens of the Baptist cause here. Repeatedly, in times of great perplexity, have the brethren solicited their aid,(144, 152) and found them ready with a hearty and effectual response. Never in a case of common or private need, through the

* He was treasurer of the church and purser for the subscribers. Nathan Tucker was collector or receiver (Ch. Rec. p. 22) until March, 1821, when Deacon Tilden took the collectorship, and Friend Crane was appointed treasurer. — (Id. p. 27.)

whole history of the church, have they failed to honor the reputation of woman for kindness of heart and cheerful helpfulness. It was they who, by their patience and faith, *held the church together* during those early feeble days, when its peaceable worship, and almost its very life, were at the mercy of an ungodly district committee.* It was they who met to pray for our Karen missionary when he was yet but a young unbeliever, and who, when he sailed for the Indies, gave material aid to his outfit. It was they who supported for years a Burman female pupil, under the name of his deceased wife.† It was they who sent substantial offerings to the young sons of the church, who had addicted themselves to the ministry, to lighten the anxieties and cheer the days of their term of study.‡ It was they who contributed largely for more than forty years, by their personal influence and combined charities, to fill up the Sunday school.§ It was they who five times generously assisted to free the church from debt. It was they who furnished and refurnished our meeting-places with the suitable appointments and conveniences of worship; and it *is* they, who, from the first, have scattered the thousand nameless donations that have comforted our parish poor, and lightened the heart of many a pastor. May the church never see the day that it shall set lightly by the modest but effectual labors of its self-denying sisters!

With a short recapitulation we close the history. No claim is made to perfect accuracy; but the following results are the best that could be made out from the existing sources of information. The church has had fourteen pastors (see p. 50, note),—BARRETT, MOORE, ADLAM, CURTIS, GEAR, MERRIAM, KIMBALL, CLARK, HOLMES, TINGLEY, FORD, RUSSELL, HERVEY, and BROWN.

The fact that Pastor Curtis was *ordained* here, and was the

* "Were it not for the faith, the confidence, and the prayers of the sisters, our church would lose its name in this world."—(Letter of Friend Crane, November, 1816, in Life of Elder Henry Kendall, p. 176.)

† Bap. Mag., vol. xvii. p. 168.

‡ See page 43; also Records Ladies' Benevolent Soc., vol. ii. p. 43.

§ Rec. Ladies' Benev. Soc., vol. i. p. 8.

first who staid for a term of years, has induced the common notion that he was the first settled pastor of the church. Perhaps Brn. Barrett, Moore, and Adlam ought only to be called *itinerant* pastors, as none of them served the church more than a year. It is difficult, however, to insist upon such a distinction merely on the ground of *time*, where *none* of the pastorates have been quite four years in duration. The character of the relation which each of these ministers here sustained to the church should be determined by the design and understanding with which he undertook it, and not by the time he staid. The taking of a residence *in response to a call* is sufficient to constitute a minister a "settled" pastor, and by this rule it is evident that the predecessors of Bro. Curtis, as also Brn. Gear and Kimball (both of whose terms were very brief), were as truly pastors as any of the rest.

The intimate connection of Brn. WILLIAMS, LINCOLN, KENDALL, and EVANS with the early history of this church, and the nature of their work here prior to the pastorate of Elder Barrett, entitles them to be called *the four apostles.*

As *special supplies*, meaning those who either received a call to the ministry here, or came *statedly* to preach for a longer or shorter time, thirty-one at least may be named,—GIBSON, BIRD, HOWARD, BENSON, JUDSON, BILLSON, THOMAS FORD, STANWOOD, ELIOT, TRACY, EWER, the HAGUES, CLEALAND, PEAK, MERRILL, DRIVER, COLEY, PEASE, CARPENTER, THOMAS, MARCHANT, DUNBAR, WILCOX, MILLER, EATON, OLMSTED, HOWELL, MASON, DEXTER, and CARR.

The *occasional* supplies I cannot undertake to enumerate. They have been a large proportion of the whole. Counting together all the preachers of every description who have addressed this people within the last half-century, we should make up a troop indeed. It is the testimony of Mr. Samuel Blackman's children, that more than a hundred different ones enjoyed the hospitalities of the "old Baptist tavern" during the first eight or ten years of the church's history. Let us hope to harvest some of the seed which these many servants of God scattered here!

There have been six deacons,*—Jason Houghton, Ezra Tilden, Friend Crane, Ezekiel Capen, George Lothrop, and Willard Shepard. Their terms of office, expressed in round numbers, have been as follows, — the first, twenty-five years; the second, sixteen years; the third, nine years; the fourth, twenty-four years; the fifth, three years; and the sixth, eighteen years. The dates of their elections and resignations are given on pages 18, 46, 58, 61, 62.

There have been seven clerks, — *Friend Crane*, the first, who served from July 1, 1814, to April, 1827,(48, 49) and again from May, 1830, till March, 1837,(102) and still again from September, 1839, to June, 1840,(116) in all about twenty-one years; *Moses Curtis*, the fourth pastor, second, who served from April, 1827, to May, 1830,(67) three years; *Asaph Merriam*, the sixth pastor, third, who served from March, 1837, to September, 1839,(112) nearly three years; *Aaron Tucker*, fourth, who served a year and three months, from June, 1840, to September, 1841; (125) *Ezekiel Capen*, fifth, who served from September, 1841, to April, 1847,(150) and again from November, 1848, to April, 1864,(232) in all about twenty-one years; *T. C. Tingley*, the tenth pastor, sixth, who served through the interval of Deacon Capen's retirement from the office, about two years;(167) and *Theron Brown*, the fourteenth pastor, seventh, who took charge of the records on the second resignation of Deacon Capen, in April, 1864.

The church has licensed three ministers, — FRANCIS MASON, CHARLES JOHNSON, and JOSEPH HODGES; and ordained three, — MOSES CURTIS, HIRAM GEAR, and DAVID B. FORD.

The whole number baptized into the fellowship of the church, during the fifty years of its life, seems to have been two hundred and twenty-four;† received by letter, seventy-nine; making, with seven restored and five re-received after

* After the resignation of Dea. Capen, April 7, 1864 (unaccepted by the church), Bro. George Coombs was elected a *third* deacon, but finally declined to serve. Dea. Capen still holds his office by request, and properly there has been no seventh deacon.

† See Appendix, p. 11.

dismission, the total of additions *three hundred and fifteen.* Forty-one have been expelled,* considerably less than one a year. Only five of these exclusions were for immorality, and, allowing the seven restorations, the number is reduced to thirty-four. Ten have been dropped, fifty-three have died in the communion, and one hundred and forty-seven have been dismissed; making, with two crossed out in the roll, unaccounted for, the total of subtractions *two hundred and fifty-three.*

Of the dismissions† from this church, 12 were to Boston: 1 to the Union Baptist Church in that city; 3 to the Harvard-street Church; 2 to the Third Baptist, or Charles-street Church; 1 to a Methodist Church; 3 to South Boston; and 2 to other parts of the city not specified. To New-York City, 5: 2 to the Tabernacle Baptist Church; 1 to Amity-street Church; 1 to the Oliver-street Church; and 1 to the new church at Williams's Bridge. To Rhode Island only 3; and to the State of Maine, 8. To New Hampshire, 2 have been dismissed; 4 to New Jersey; 3 to Pennsylvania; 2 to Connecticut; 1 to Iowa; and 2 to New Brunswick. To churches in Massachusetts, exclusive of Boston, there have been dismissed 101: 2 to the Unitarian Church at Canton Corner; 2 to Stoughton; 5 to East Dedham; 2 to South Dedham; 5 to Sharon; 4 to Foxboro'; 7 to Dorchester; 3 to Sheldonville (Wrentham); 6 to Wrentham town; 8 to Randolph; 4 to Middleboro'; 1 to Taunton; 1 to Neponset; 7 to Roxbury; 1 to Hingham; 1 to Hanover; 1 to Marshfield; 2 to Medfield; 2 to East Cambridge; 2 to Mansfield; 1 to Attleboro'; 1 to Sturbridge; 1 to Ware; 1 to Medford; 1 to Brewster; 2 to Becket; 6 to Lowell; 1 to Salisbury and Amesbury; 1 to East Medway; 4 to Athol; 1 to Braintree; 1 to Winthrop; 2 to Warren;‡ 1 to Holden; 1 to Winchester; 1 to Pittsfield; 1 to Woburn; 2 to Fall River; 2 to Worcester; 2 to South

* Under expulsions, I include all names recorded as "*erased.*"

† I include under dismissions, *certificates of character and standing.* I believe there are but five or six cases of that description.

‡ Worcester County.

Hanson; and 2 to Charlestown. Four of the dismissions are without designation. The number at present in the communion is *ninety-seven.**

It may be added that the church has participated in eighteen councils: in *Canton*, on the 22d of June, 1814, at its own constitution; in *Sharon*, June, 1818, to ordain Samuel Waitt, by delegates Jason Houghton, Ezra Tilden, and Friend Crane (21); in *North Randolph*, October, 1819, to constitute the Baptist Church there, by delegate Jason Houghton (25); in *Canton*, Aug. 29, 1827, to ordain Moses Curtis (51); in *Canton*, April 11, 1832, to ordain Hiram Gear (82); in *East Randolph*, May 10, 1836, to constitute a church there, by delegates Rev. —— Burlingame, Friend Crane, and Ralph H. Crane (100); in *Sharon*, May, 1837, to ordain George N. Waitt, by delegates Benjamin Gill and Pastor Merriam (103); in *Needham*, September, 1837, to constitute the Baptist Church there, by delegates Jason Houghton and Pastor Merriam (106); in *Boston*, Sept. 20, 1839, to depose Charles O. Kimball, by delegates E. Capen and (?) Friend Crane (113); in *Roxbury*, Feb. 23, 1848, to divide the Boston Association, by delegates Willard Shepard, William Pettengill, E. Capen, and Pastor Tingley (158); in *North Randolph*, June 8, 1848, to ordain R. W. E. Brown, by delegates Benjamin Gill, James White, and Pastor Tingley (165); in *Canton*, Sept. 25, 1851, to ordain David B. Ford, by delegates E. Capen, W. Shepard, and A. E. Tucker (178); in *Mansfield*, Sept. 29, 1852,† to ordain Welcome Lewis, by delegates W. Shepard, George Wiswall, and Pastor Ford (186); in *Boston*, May 24, 1854, to advise on the erection of a Seaman's Chapel, by delegates W. Shepard and E. Capen (193); in *East Dedham*, April 20, 1857, to advise for an aggrieved member, by delegates A. E. Tucker and Pastor Russell (204); in *South Braintree*, July, 1858, to advise on dividing the Baptist Church there, by delegates A. E. Tucker and Pastor Hervey (212); in

* Dec. 31, 1864.

† Records have "North Bridgewater" erased, and "Mansfield" written over on page 185, and on page 186 "Mansfield" erased, and "North Bridgewater" written over. Report of Bap. Mass. Convention, 1852, has "Mansfield, September 30."

South Dedham, Nov. 3, 1858, to constitute the Baptist Church there, by delegates A. E. Tucker and William Cobbet (214); and in *East Stoughton*, Jan. 8, 1861, to examine charges against a member, by delegates E. Capen and Pastor Hervey.

Thus we come to the end — and yet not the end; for, with immortal beings like ourselves, there is always something after the end.

Throughout this recital, we have been in communication with the spirits of the fathers, and they have told us how they built, and how we must build,—how patiently as well as how speedily, how cautiously as well as how much.

We are to take up the history of this church where they left it, and add *our* chapter to the half century that has already been lived and written. Their example can teach us much that we shall then have no need to learn by bitter experience; and if we take care not to undermine the foundation they laid here, or undo a single advantage that they gained in the long term of their toil, the chances are that fifty years from now, this church will stand like Lebanon, waving fresh and broad and high with the fruits of the first "handful of corn."

If this brief study of our past history here, to-day, shall serve to spur us every one to add something noble ourselves to those early efforts which the Lord blessed, and each contribute some new joy to the happiness of that centennial jubilee, this Memorial Sermon will not have been written in vain. By it, the faithful appeals of every pastor who has honored the ministry among you are called to remembrance, and listened to once more. Let them not be soon forgotten. And here we should kindly remember that the labors of these good men are not to be judged solely by the *marked revivals* which attended them. In the history of a church, revivals are, to be sure, *prima facie* evidence of the divine blessing; but they are not, as we have seen, necessarily proof of the highest spiritual health and strength. Estimated by these, our own church, which has enjoyed, on an average, but about one in every ten years of her existence, could be said to have been but five or six times in a condition of prosperity during her fifty years, which is short of the truth. Excepting the mournful relapse between 1842 and 1851, conversions and additions by baptism have continued at intervals of rarely more than a year, and never more than two years. A steady glow of life and love is better than periodical fervor and power. The latter is the strength of Samson; the former is the strength of Christ. For His strength let us pray; to attain that, let us gather wisdom from the counsels and toils of our departed saints.

So it may happen to us as it did to the church in Babylon, when the old records of the kingdom were reviewed, and they set about building the Holy City; for it is written that they "*builded and prospered through the prophesying of Haggai the prophet, and Zechariah the son of Iddo; and they builded and finished it according to the commandment of the God of Israel.*"

Our church has had its Haggais and Zechariahs, and prospered through their prophesying. May it build and prosper through the prophesying of its present pastor! "Let the foundations be strongly laid . . . with three rows of great stones and a row of new timber; and let the expenses be given out of the King's house."

MEMORIAL VERSES.

THE VALLEY CHURCH.

By the green feet of bold Blue Hill,
Neponset's vagrant river flows ;.
And on his meadowy margin still
The ancient blossoms ope and close.
The lakelets whence his waters rose
Dimple the distant landscape yet,
And, leaping as of old, to fill
His billowy bosom where they met.
Down from the Sharon uplands sweet,
And east through Ponkapog ravine,
O'er the same beds of mossy green,
And sparkling with their wonted gleams,
Fall Massapoag and Pekameet,
His children with their tribute-streams.
  Unchanged for picturesque repose
(By eye of bird remotely scanned),
The winding of the waters shows,
And likeness of the swelling land.
  Unchanged as these in faith and will,
A Christian tribe that vale have trod,
Through fifty years of good and ill,
A humble, hated church of God.
Still clear in ancient breadth and length,
Their healthful doctrines flow and run ;
And round, like living hills of strength,
Stand the old truths whose war they won :
While as each season comes and goes,
And months of cheer succeed to chill,

Blooms haply now the gospel rose,
And lilies fleck the fields they till.
Unchanged. The stealthy wand of time
Hath spared the salient shapes of prime;
But finer tokens under those
To closer gaze proclaim the new,
That 'scapes the stranger's hasty view.
O'er lake-fed river, brook, and rill,
By rocks the Indian fisher chose,
The bridge its useful level throws,
And busy hums the laboring mill.
The forest, cleft with axe and bill,
Lets through apace the screaming car
By olden farm and domicil,
And hamlet up the valley far,
Where later work of wealth and skill
Hath stocked the fathers' rude domain
With marts of trade and shrines of gain.

So, borne by viewless social force,
The holders of a changeless creed,
Through fifty summers' gliding course,
Have tracked the changing ways of need.

So, in the turns of death and life
That shift the generations, they
Have changed the leaders of their strife,
And laid the heroic sires away.

The moss-grown dome, where first they met
By the old road, is standing yet;
And near the landmark-mountain high,
The small brown schoolhouse, where in days
Of struggling hope they sung God's praise,
Waits while the years of time go by;
And southward, on the central grounds,
Their first plain temple's modest walls
Record the holy sights and sounds
Of Zion's early festivals.

But in yon graveyard's grassy breast,
The balsam and the tufted larch
Sigh o'er the saints who paused to rest
Beneath them in their earthly march;
And farther south, where field and stream
Show thick with forge and village-home,
The white church, manse, and chapel gleam,
And there to-day their children come.

Farewell, good pilgrims! Though the sneer
Of pride condemned your doctrines here,
In proofs your foes survive to give,
Your labors and your witness live.

Ye had your trials and complaints,
Your fight with olden errors taught,
When scoffers, with the name of saints,
Would frown you from the rights ye bought:
Ye had your sad Egyptian days,
Your midnight sea, your desert maze,
Till He whose grace our patience fills
Conveyed you to his heavenly hills.

We look for triumph through your pain
And ours, who yet the fight maintain,
Where Midian with his guileful band
Detains us from the promised land.

Church of the valley! ne'er forget
Thy first espousals! Lo! the seal
Thy Saviour on thy forehead set,
That bridal morning — sacred yet —
Assures thy heart with mute appeal
The utmost love a God can feel.
That pledge remember, and the hour
Of happy faith and holy pride,
When thou in weakness, He in power,
Walked first this garden side by side.

What matter though thy story fail
Of large event and action rare?
The limits of a village tale
Are large enough with JESUS there.
And somewhat thou hast known of Him,
Through all thy weak and erring years,
To stay thee yet when love is dim,
To light thy way when lost in tears.

Grow wise by thought of follies past;
Grow strong by hope of better things;
But make thy Lord thy first and last,
And seek the shadow of his wings.

O, long as glide those wand'ring waves
By bold Blue Mountain's verdant feet,
And oft as smiling spring-time paves
Those mossy meads with blossoms sweet,
So long, O child of fifty springs,
Thy life, though devious, fruitful flow;
So oft thy garden and thy king's,
Church of the valley, bud and blow!

APPENDIX.

CREED AND COVENANT.

The Canton Church cannot be said to have changed her creed, but she has altered her *expression* of it twice. The original Declaration of Faith appears to have been used until 1843, when, on the 5th of March, another, slightly differing in phraseology, but the same in sentiment and doctrine, was adopted from the Sharon Church (Ch. Rec. p. 138). This creed was retained a little more than ten years, after which the following more perfect form, with the accompanying covenant from the "Hand-Book" of Rev. Dr. Crowell, was adopted, and is now the accepted Declaration of Faith, of this, as of many other Baptist Churches in New England.

ARTICLES OF CHRISTIAN BELIEF.

I. OF THE SCRIPTURES.

We believe the Holy Bible was written by men divinely inspired, and is a perfect treasure of heavenly instruction; that it has God for its author, salvation for its end, and truth, without any mixture of error, for its matter; that it reveals the principles by which God will judge us; and therefore is, and shall remain to the end of the world, the true centre of Christian union, and the supreme standard by which all human conduct, creeds, and opinions should be tried.

II. OF THE TRUE GOD.

That there is one, and only one, true and living God, whose name is Jehovah, the Maker and Supreme Ruler of heaven and earth; inexpressibly glorious in holiness; worthy of all possible honor, confidence, and love; revealed under the personal and relative distinctions of the Father, the Son, and the Holy Spirit; equal in every divine perfection, and executing distinct but harmonious offices in the great work of redemption.

III. OF THE FALL OF MAN.

That man was created in a state of holiness under the law of his Maker, but by voluntary transgression fell from that holy and happy state; in consequence of which all mankind are now sinners, not by constraint, but choice, being by nature utterly void of that holiness required by the law of God, wholly given to the gratification of the world, of Satan, and of their own sinful passions, and therefore under just condemnation to eternal ruin, without defence or excuse.

IV. THE WAY OF SALVATION.

That the salvation of sinners is wholly of *grace;* through the mediatorial offices of the Son of God, who took upon him our nature, yet without sin; honored the law by his personal obedience, and made atonement for our sins by his death; being risen from the dead, he is now enthroned in heaven; and, uniting in his wonderful person the tenderest sympathies with divivine perfections, is every way qualified to be a suitable, a compassionate, and an all-sufficient Saviour.

V. OF JUSTIFICATION.

That the great Gospel blessing which Christ of his fulness bestows on such as believe in Him is Justification; that Justification consists in the pardon of sin and the promise of eternal life, on principles of righteousness; that it is bestowed, not in consideration of any works of righteousness which we have done, but solely through His own redemption and righteousness; that it brings us into a state of most blessed peace and favor with God, and secures every other blessing needful for time and eternity.

VI. OF THE FREENESS OF SALVATION.

That the blessings of salvation are made free to all by the Gospel; that it is the immediate duty of all to accept them by a cordial and obedient faith; and that nothing prevents the salvation of the greatest sinner on earth, except his own voluntary refusal to submit to the Lord Jesus Christ, which refusal will subject him to an aggravated condemnation.

VII. OF GRACE IN REGENERATION.

That in order to be saved, we must be *regenerated*, or born again; that Regeneration consists in giving a holy disposition to the mind, and is effected in a manner above our comprehension or calculation, by the power of the Holy Spirit, so as to secure our voluntary obedience to the Gospel; and that its proper evidence is found in the holy fruit which we bring forth to the glory of God.

VIII. OF GOD'S PURPOSE OF GRACE.

That Election is the gracious purpose of God, according to which he regenerates, sanctifies, and saves sinners; that being perfectly consistent with the free agency of man, it comprehends all the means in connection with the end; that it is a most glorious display of God's sovereign goodness, being infinitely wise, holy, and unchangeable; that it utterly excludes boasting, and promotes humility, prayer, praise, trust in God, and active imitation of his free mercy; that it encourages the use of means in the highest degree; that it is ascertained by its effects in all who believe the gospel; is the foundation of Christian assurance; and that to ascertain it with regard to ourselves, demands and deserves our utmost diligence.

IX. OF THE PERSEVERANCE OF SAINTS.

That such only are real believers as endure unto the end; that their persevering attachment to Christ is the grand mark which distinguishes them from mere professors; that a special Providence watches over their welfare; and they are kept by the power of God, through faith unto salvation.

X. HARMONY OF THE LAW AND GOSPEL.

That the law of God is the eternal and unchangeable rule of his moral government; that it is holy, just, and good; and that the inability which the Scriptures ascribe to fallen men to fulfil its precepts, arises entirely from their love of sin; to deliver them from which, and to restore them through a Mediator to unfeigned obedience to the holy law, is one great end of the Gospel, and of the means of grace connected with the establishment of the visible church.

XI. OF A GOSPEL CHURCH.

That a visible church of Christ is a congregation of baptized believers, associated by covenant in the faith and fellowship of the Gospel, observing the ordinances of Christ, governed by his laws, and exercising the gifts, rights, and privileges invested in them by his word; that its only proper officers are Bishops or Pastors, and Deacons, whose qualifications, claims, and duties are defined in the Epistles to Timothy and Titus.

XII. OF BAPTISM AND THE LORD'S SUPPER.

That Christian Baptism is the immersion of a believer in water, in the name of the Father, Son, and Spirit, to show forth in a solemn and beautiful emblem our faith in a crucified, buried, and risen Saviour, with its purifying power; that it is pre-requisite to the privileges of a church relation, and to the Lord's Supper, in which the members of the church, by the use of bread and wine, are to commemorate together the dying love of Christ; preceded always by a solemn self-examination.

XIII. OF THE CHRISTIAN SABBATH.

That the first day of the week is the Lord's Day, or Christian Sabbath, and is to be kept sacred to religious purposes, by abstaining from all secular labor and recreations; by the devout observance of all the means of grace, both private and public; and by preparation for that rest which remaineth for the people of God.

XIV. OF CIVIL GOVERNMENT.

That civil government is of divine appointment, for the interests and good order of human society; and that magistrates are to be prayed for, conscientiously honored, and obeyed, except in things opposed to the will of our Lord Jesus Christ, who is the only Lord of the conscience, and the Prince of the kings of earth.

XV. OF THE RIGHTEOUS AND THE WICKED.

That there is a radical and essential difference between the righteous and the wicked; that such only as through faith are justified in the name of the Lord Jesus, and sanctified by the Spirit of our God, are truly righteous in his esteem; while all such as continue in impenitence and unbelief are in his sight wicked, and under the curse; and this distinction holds among men both in and after death.

XVI. OF THE WORLD TO COME.

That the end of this world is approaching; that at the last day, Christ will descend from heaven, and raise the dead from the grave to final retribution; that a solemn separation will then take place; that the wicked will be adjudged to endless punishment, and the righteous to endless joy; and that this judgment will fix forever the final state of men in heaven or hell, on principles of righteousness.

CHURCH COVENANT.

As we trust we have been brought by divine grace to embrace the Lord Jesus Christ, and by the influence of his Spirit to give ourselves up to him, so we do now solemnly covenant with each other, that, God enabling us, we will walk together in brotherly love.

That we will exercise a Christian care and watchfulness over each other, and faithfully warn, rebuke, and admonish one another, as the case shall require.

That we will not forsake the assembling of ourselves together, nor omit the great duty of prayer, both for ourselves and for others.

That we will participate in each other's joys, and endeavor with tenderness and sympathy to bear each other's burdens and sorrows.

That we will earnestly endeavor to bring up such as may be under our care in the nurture and admonition of the Lord.

That we will seek divine aid to enable us to walk circumspectly and watchfully in the world, denying ungodliness and every worldly lust.

That we will strive together for the support of a faithful evangelical ministry among us.

That we will endeavor, by example and effort, to win souls to Christ.

And through life, amidst evil report and good report, seek to live to the glory of Him who hath called us out of darkness into his marvellous light.

Table of Pastorates, Ages, etc.

The following are the names of the apostles and pastors of Canton Baptist Church, with time of visit, or term of service, and time of death and age attached to each.*

NAME.	Was here statedly, or occasionally.	Died.	Age.
1. WILLIAMS	1812–27	Feb. 1845	77
2. LINCOLN	1813–21	Dec. 1832	53
3. KENDALL	1814–17	Aug. 1864	90
4. EVANS	1817, 1823, 1825–26	Jan. 1848	53

NAME.	Came.	Went.	Length of Pastorate.	Died.	Age.
1. BARRETT	Jan.? 1821	Mar.? 1822	1 yr. 2 mos.	Aug. 1832	40
2. MOORE	July, 1824	June, 1825	11 mos.	Apr. 1858	61
3. ADLAM	Sept. 1826	Mar.? 1827	5 mos.	. .	68
4. CURTIS	Aug. 1827	May, 1830	2 yrs. 10 mos.	. .	71
5. GEAR	Oct. 1831	Dec. 1832	1 yr. 1 mo.	Feb. 1843	38
6. MERRIAM	Sept. 1836	Sept. 1839	3 yrs.	. .	74
7. KIMBALL	Sept. 1839	Nov. 1839	6 weeks?	July, 1854	62
8. CLARK	Apr. 1840	June, 1842	2 yrs. 2 mos.	. .	55
9. HOLMES	June, 1843	Nov. 1844	1 yr. 5 mos.	. .	53
10. TINGLEY	May, 1845	Nov. 1848	3 yrs. 6 mos.†	. .	62
11. FORD	May, 1851	Nov. 1853	2 yrs. 6 mos.	. .	46
12. RUSSELL	Apr. 1854	July, 1857	3 yrs. 3 mos.	. .	59
13. HERVEY	Feb. 1858	July, 1861	3 yrs. 5 mos.	. .	44
14. BROWN	Mar. 1863	. .	3 yrs. 4 mos.‡	. .	34‡

* The pastoral terms in this Table are not intended to include *supplies before settlement.*

† Mr. Tingley's pastorate was the longest of any, exceeding Mr. Hervey's by a little over a month. Mr. Kimball's was the shortest.

‡ To June, 1866. The *ages* are all reckoned down to June, 1866.

Table of the Names and Dates of Special Pulpit Supplies of the Canton Baptist Church during the last half century.

Howard	1816
Gibson	1816
Bird	1817
Judson (about)	1818
Billson (about)	1820
Benson (about)	1822
Ford	1822
Stanwood	1823
Eliot	1823–24
Tracy	1825
Ewer	1830
Hague, Wm. (about)	1830
Clealand	1831
Peak	1831
Merrill	1831
Driver, Thos. (about)	1831
Coley	1831–33
Pease	1833
Carpenter	1833
Marchant	1833–34
Thomas	1833
Hague, John B.	1834
Dunbar	1835
Wilcox	1835
Miller	1839
Eaton	1842–43
Olmsted	1848–51
Howell	1857
Mason	1861–62
Dexter	1862
Carr	1862–63

Table of Expenditures of the Baptist Church in Canton during its first Fifty Years.

*** An unusually large sum falling to any year, in the business list, generally indicates that at that date a building was erected or repaired, or a considerable debt paid.

*** The list of *charities* comprises donations to Home and Foreign Missions, Educational Societies and Institutions, pastors and needy church-members, and *all* contributions (in aid of the church as well as of general religious interests) made by the Sunday School and the Ladies' Benevolent Society.

YEAR.	Preaching.	Current Expenses, &c.	Charities.	Total.
1814	$50 00?	$5 00	..	$55 00
1815	75 00?	7 50	..	82 50
1816	75 00?	25 00?	..	100 00
1817	75 00?	25 00?	..	100 00
1818	75 00?	25 00?	..	100 00
1819	75 00?	25 00?	..	100 00
1820	150 00	105 00	$5 00	260 00
1821	200 00	2,025 00	10 00	2,235 00
1822	300 00	30 00?	..	330 00
1823	300 00	30 00?	..	330 00
1824	300 00	30 00?	..	330 00
1825	300 00	30 00?	..	330 00
1826	300 00	68 00	10 00	378 00
1827	350 00	50 00	..	400 00
1828	350 00	30 00?	..	380 00
1829	350 00	40 00?	77 00	467 00
1830	300 00	40 00?	11 00	361 00
1831	270 00	40 00?	52 00	362 00
1832	245 00	40 00?	54 37	339 37
Amounts carried forward	$4,140 00	$2,670 50	$219 37	$7,039 87

Table of Expenditures.—Continued.

YEAR.	Preaching.	Current Expenses, &c.	Charities.	Total.
Amounts brought forward	$4,140 00	$2,670 50	$219 37	$7,039 87
1833	350 00	44 39	36 00	430 39
1834	260 00	40 00	36 00	336 00
1835	260 00	270 00	36 00	566 00
1836	260 00	3,340 00	16 00	3,616 00
1837	500 00	432 00	33 00	965 00
1838	500 00	333 95	16 00	849 95
1839	560 00	77 00	11 00	648 00
1840	700 00	100 00	173 00	973 00
1841	700 00	1,665 79	25 45	2,391 24
1842	395 00	467 05	60 89	922 94
1843	500 00	273 83	61 58	834 58
1844	450 00	60 00	48 00	558 00
1845	448 00	267 50	26 00	741 50
1846	500 00	80 00	29 00	609 00
1847	475 00	270 76	54 00	799 76
1848	405 00	248 35	157 38	810 73
1849	250 00	133 94	32 00	415 94
1850	255 00	801 97	12 00	1,068 97
1851	302 00	185 28	29 16	516 44
1852	439 00	153 62	18 15	610 77
1853	600 00	115 37	221 14	936 51
1854	341 00	124 39	151 47	616 86
1855	450 00	1,130 88	150 37	1,731 25
1856	462 00	138 18	150 88	751 06
1857	408 00	142 84	177 26	728 10
1858	550 00	191 82	93 33	835 15
1859	400 00	144 45	185 20	729 65
1860	444 00	118 44	127 94	690 38
1861	755 00	180 64	114 27	1,049 91
1862	450 00	2,013 54	68 62	2,532 16
1863	482 00	91 67	90 52	664 19
1864	600 00*	492 00	267 06	1,359 06

Besides the recorded charities, donations (unrecorded) have been made for ministerial education, for feeble churches, and other benevolent objects at different times, amounting to no less than six hundred dollars, by a member of the church, whose Christian liberality has made him known far beyond the limits of his own town. Counting this with others, the sum of the church charities is $3,528 04; and with this in its column, the result from the whole table appears as follows:—

Expenses for the fifty years; several and grand totals to Dec. 31, 1864 . .	$18,591 00	$16,890 15	$3,528 04	$39,009 19

* The rent of the parsonage, reckoned into the salary since 1841, does not appear in the table.

Table of Statistics of Membership, Loss, Gain, etc.

The number of baptisms cannot be absolutely certified. The total of additions is easily ascertained by deducting the original number, 35, from 350, the whole number of members in the church, between June 22, 1814, and Dec. 31, 1864. But the roll on which we depend for these general data makes no intelligible distinction of the admissions by baptism from those by letter; and the account of these in the records is shown to be defective: for, adding together the 222 baptisms and 76 admissions by letter, recorded there, we obtain for the whole number of additions, even with the 7 restored and the 5 re-received after dismission, only 310; less by 5 than the true total of additions, which is 315. Distributing the 5 to the two uncertain numbers, we make out, by the fairest method that seems to be left us, 224 admissions by baptism and 79 by letter. The following is a synopsis of the statistics of the loss and gain of the church during the fifty years.

LOSS.

Dismissed	147
Died	53
Excluded	41
Dropped	10
Crossed out on roll, not accounted for	2
	253

GAIN.

Baptized	224
Received by letter	79
Restored	7
Re-admitted after dismission	5
	315

VERIFICATIONS.

35 Original number of members,
97 Present number of members,
350 Grand total of membership, } Known terms.

350 — 35 = 315: total of additions.
350 — 97 = 253: total of subtractions.
315 — 253 + 35 = 97: present number.

List of Names of all the Persons who have belonged to the Canton Baptist Church between June 22, 1814, and July 24, 1865.

A.

Adams, Nancy.
Allen, Lucy.
Ames, Julia R. (Crane).*

B.

Bartlett, Julia.
Beals, Amasa.
Beals, Mary.
Beals, William.
Beaumont, Irene.
Belcher, Clifford.
Belcher, Elizabeth.
Belcher, Mary.
Belcher, Rebecca.
Belcher, Sardy.
Bense, Charlotte E.
Bense, Elizabeth P.
Bense, William.
Bent, Joseph.
Billings, Eliza.
Blackman, Abigail.
Blackman, Samuel.
Blaisdell, Orrison.
Blake, Clara.
Blake, Clara, 2d.
Bliss, Mary.
Boswell, Thomas.
Boswell, Anna.
Bourne, David.
Bourne, Sarah Ann.
Bray, Isabella J.
Bray, Sarah (Crane).
Bright, Alvirah.
Brooks, Jane.
Brown, Emeline.
Brown, Helen M.
Brown, Theron.
Bryant, Charles.
Bullard, Maria B.
Bullard, Mary E.
Bullard, William.
Burnham, Julia M. (Shepard.)
Buss, Sally (or Ruth).

C.

Capen, Emma P. (Knaggs.)
Capen, Ezekiel.
Capen, Mary (Brett).
Carpenter, Hannah.
Carr, Hiram.
Carroll, Emily C.
Ceiley, Catharine L.
Ceiley, Mary.
Chamberlain, George E.
Chandler, Ann Jane (Withington).
Clark, Henry.
Clark, John.
Clark, (Mrs.)
Cobb, Adeline.
Cobb, Rachel (Ward).
Cobbet, Joanna.
Cobbet, Rachel F.
Cobbet, Susan (Smith).
Cobbet, William.
Cook, Orinda.

* The parentheses enclose *maiden* names.

Coombs, Catharine E.
Coombs, George.
Coombs, John.
Crane, Abby.
Crane, Clara.
Crane, Elizabeth.
Crane, Esther.
Crane, Friend.
Crane, Lucy.
Crane, Ralph H.
Crane, Rebecca.
Crane, Richard Stoddard.
Crane, Seth.
Crane, Susan.
Croud, Daniel.
Croud, Daniel W.
Croud, Betsy S.
Croud, Mary E.
Culver, David.
Currier, Samuel.
Curtis, Mary Arnold.
Curtis, Moses.
Cutler, Henrietta (Tucker).

D.

Damon, Mary.
Davenport, Hannah (Tucker).
Davis, Nathaniel Tucker.
Dean, Mary.
Dickerman, Mary A. (Hunt.)
Drake, Alice B.
Drake, Charles.
Drake, Susan (Holmes).
Dumphy, Ellen M. (Withington.)
Dunbar, Darius.

E.

Emmerton, Elizabeth.
Emmerton, Cath. (Chamberlain.)
Endicott, Cynthia.
Endicott, Elijah.
Esty, Clinton.

F.

Fadden, Andrew.
Fadden, (Mrs.)
Fales, Nancy.
Farrington, Charles.
Farrington, David.
Farrington, (Mrs.)
Fisher, Bethiah (Tilden).
Fisher, Clarissa (Cobb).
Fisher, Henry.
Fisher, Mary (Upham).
Ford, David B.
Foster, Sarah (Crane).
French, Joanna.
Fuller, Bathsheba.
Fuller, Emily C.
Fuller, Lemuel.
Fuller, Oliver P.
Fuller, Rebecca.

G.

Gage, Eveline (Belcher).
Gay, Elizabeth.
George, Amos D.
Gerald, Ruth (McKendry).
Gill, Abigail.
Gill, Abigail (Bird).
Gill, Benjamin.
Gill, Rebekah.
Gould, Catharine.
Gould, Charlotte.
Graves, Mary E. (Davis.)
Gray, Sarah Ann.
Gurney, Ellen.

H.

Hardman, Ann.
Hardman, Charles F.

Hawes, Elijah.
Heald, Sarah (Pettengill).
Hersey, Lorra A. (Upham).
Heustis, Elizabeth (Brooks).
Hill, Abigail.
Hill, Eleanor (Crane).
Hixon, Hannah.
Hodges, Joseph.
Hodges, Joseph, 2d.
Hodges, Sally.
Hodges, Sarah.
Holmes, Mary E. (Carpenter.)
Houghton, Caty.
Houghton, Charles W.
Houghton, Jason.
Houghton, Mary.
Houghton, Oliver.
Houghton, Ruth.
Hunt, I. Newton.
Hunt, Jerusha N.
Hunt, Mary.
Hunt, Polly (Bryant).
Hunt, Ruth.
Hunt, Sophia S.
Hunt, Warren.

I.

Ingraham, Caroline.

J.

Jackman, Lucy Jane.
Jewell, Elizabeth.
Johnson, Charles.
Johnson, Elizabeth.
Johnson, Elizabeth, 2d.
Johnson, Ellen (Tilden).
Johnson, Hannah (Wood).
Johnson, Mary.

K.

Kaley, Sarah (Upham).
Keith, Mary E.
Kelso, Jonathan G.
Kelso, Sarah.
Kenrick, Elizabeth.
Kenrick, Julia A.
Kenrick, Susannah C.
Kent, Mary C.
Kent, Sarah.
Kimball, Charles O.
Kimball, Elizabeth.
Kimball, Mary (Tilden).
Kinsley, Sarah (Belcher).
Knaggs, Elizabeth.
Knight, Sarah (Palmer).

L.

Lacy, David.
Lathrop, Abigail (Tilden).
Leach, Clementina D.
Leach, Elbridge G.
Leonard, Ruth.
Lessure, Hannah.
Littlefield, Betsey.
Littlefield, Julia (Tucker).
Locke, Nancy (Spare).
Lopez, Mary (Tilden).
Lord, Elizabeth (Brett).
Lothrop, George H.
Lothrop, William.
Loud, Lydia.
Low, Edmund.
Low, Fally Jane.

M.

McPherson, Hugh.
Makepeace, Harriet (White).
Mann, Hepzibah.
Mann, Isaac.
Marden, Charles W.
Marden, Eliza.
Mason, Eveline (Knaggs).
Mason, Francis.

Mason, Lucinda (Gill).
May, Clarissa (Wentworth).
Merriam, Asaph.
Merriam, Lorana.
Messenger, Howard C.
Messenger, Sarah.
Miner, Louisa (Tucker).
Morse, Nancy.
Morse, Ruth.
Munro, Ruth.

N.

Nelson, Amariah C.
Nickerson, Eunice.
Nutting, Sarah.

P.

Petit, Elizabeth (Bailey).
Pettengill, Sally.
Pettengill, William.
Pickernell, Lucy.
Pierce, Roby.
Pike, Mary (Morse).
Pitcher, Joanna (French).
Pope, Ann.
Pope, William.

R.

Randall, Clara (Upham).
Randall, Mary.
Richardson, Lucy (Johnson).
Richardson, Mary A.
Roberts, Ann E.
Russell, Catharine (Brailey).
Russell, Elizabeth.
Russell, Philemon R.
Russell, ———

S.

Sanborn, Caroline.
Savels, Abigail.
Searfoss, Margaret.
Seaward, Alfred.
Seckel, Elmira (Snow).
Shaw, Elmira.
Shaw, Vesta.
Shepard, Frances.
Shepard, Harriet.
Shepard, Harriet B.
Shepard, Julia Ann.
Shepard, Sarah.
Shepard, Willard.
Shepardson, Nancy.
Shorey, Catharine.
Simmons, Benjamin.
Sinclair, Joanna (Taunt).
Smith, Caroline.
Smith, Caroline E.
Smith, Emila (Hamilton).
Smith, Howard.
Smith, Jane.
Smith, Sarah.
Smith, Timothy.
Smith, Zeba.
Snow, Abigail.
Snow, Abigail, 2d.
Snow, Ebenezer.
Snow, Jane.
Snow, Naomi.
Spare, Elijah.
Spare, Sally.
Spare, Sarah Ann.
Sprague, Ellen.
Standish, Harriet (Loud).
Stimpson, Mary.
Stoddard, Betsy (Tucker).

T.

Talbot, Lucinda T.
Taylor, Elizabeth.
Thompson, Harriet (Drake).
Tilden, Abner.

Tilden Bethiah.
Tilden, Catharine.
Tilden, Ezra.
Tilden, Hannah (Gill).
Tilden, Julia.
Tilden, Lemuel.
Tilden, Mary.
Tingley, Nancy B.
Tingley, Timothy C.
Tisdale, Alice.
Tobey, Nancy (White).
Tucker, Aaron E.
Tucker, Annie.
Tucker, Caty.
Tucker, Eliza.
Tucker, Eliza Ann.
Tucker, Elizabeth.
Tucker, Elizabeth, 2d.
Tucker, Elizabeth, 3d.
Tucker, Ellen (Kenrick).
Tucker, Eunice.
Tucker, George.
Tucker, Hannah.
Tucker, Isaac.
Tucker, Mary G.
Tucker, Mary (Houghton).
Tucker, Milla.
Tucker, Nathan.
Tucker, Nathan, 2d.
Tucker, Olive.
Tucker, Olive H.
Tucker, Samuel.

U.

Upham, Charles.
Upham, Enos.
Upham, Enos, 2d.
Upham, Eveline (Endicott).
Upham, Rebecca.
Upham, Sarah.

W.

Weed, George A.
Wentworth, Jane.
Wentworth, Jane, 2d.
Wentworth, Sarah (Bright).
Wheeler, Eliphal.
White, Aurelia.
White, James.
White, Sally.
Whitehouse, Mar. C. (Withington).
Wild, Jonathan.
Wild, Relief.
Williams, Eliza Jane (Hunt).
Wiswall, Elizabeth (Briggs).
Wiswall, Emily.
Wiswall, George M.
Wiswall, John.
Wiswall, Joseph.
Wiswall, Lewis.
Wiswall, Lois.
Wiswall, Mehitabel.
Wiswall, Pamelia.
Withington, Enos.
Withington, Lucinda.
Withington, Mary.
Withington, Sarah.
Withington, Susan.
Withington, Wales.
Wood, James M.
Wood, Sarah Ann.
Worthington, Albert.
Worthington, Caroline.
Wright, Desire.
Wright, George C.
Wright, Olive B.

Total, 350.

Alphabetical List of the Present Members of the Canton Baptist Church, July 24, 1865.

Ames, Julia R. (Crane).

Beals, Amasa.
Beals, Mary.
Belcher, Elizabeth.
Belcher, Mary.
Bense, Elizabeth P.
Bense, Charlotte E.
Bense, William.
Billings, Eliza.
Blake, Clara.
Bray, Sarah (Crane).*
Brown, Helen M.
Brown, Theron.
Bullard, Maria B.
Bullard, Mary E.
Bullard, William.
Burnham, Julia M. (Shepard).

Capen, Emma P.
Capen, Ezekiel.
Carroll, Emily C.
Carpenter, Hannah.
Chandler, Ann J. (Withington).
Cobbet, Joanna.
Cobbet, Rachel F.
Cobbet, William.
Coombs, Catharine E.
Coombs, George.
Coombs, John.
Crane, Clara.
Croud, Daniel.
Croud, Mary E.

Dunbar, Frances (Shepard).

Emmerton, Cath.(Chamberl'n).
Emmerton, Elizabeth.
Endicott, Cynthia.
Esty, Clinton.

Fisher, Clarissa Cobb.

Gill, Benjamin.
Gill, Rebekah.

Hardman, Charles F.†
Holmes, Mary E. (Carpenter).
Hunt, Polly (Bryant).
Hunt, Sophia S.

Johnson, Ellen (Tilden).

Kenrick, Elizabeth.
Kenrick, Julia A.
Kenrick, Susannah C.
Keith, Mary E.
Knaggs, Elizabeth.

Leach, Clementina D.
Leach, Elbridge G.

McPherson, Hugh.
Mason, Francis.
Miner, Louisa (Tucker).

Nutting, Sarah.

* Dismissed, Jan. 7, 1866.

† Dismissed, Nov. 6, 1865.

Pettengill, William.
Pitcher, Joanna (French).

Randall, Clara (Upham).
Richardson Lucy (Johnson).
Russell, Catharine (Brailey).

Shaw, Elmira C.
Shaw, Vesta.
Shepard, Harriet B.
Shepard, Julia Ann.
Shepard, Willard.
Sinclair, Joanna (Taunt).
Smith, Sarah.
Snow, Naomi.
Sprague, Ellen.
Stimpson, Mary.

Taylor, Elizabeth.
Tilden, Catharine.

Tucker, Aaron E.
Tucker, Annie.
Tucker, Ellen (Kenrick).
Tucker, Eunice.
Tucker, Hannah.
Tucker, Mary (Houghton).

Upham, Eveline (Endicott).

White, Aurelia.
White, James.*
Whitehouse, Marg't C. (Withington).
Williams, Eliza Jane (Hunt).
Withington, Enos.
Wiswall, Elizabeth (Briggs).
Wiswall, Joseph.
Wright, George C.
Wright, Desire.
Wright, Olive B.

N. B. *Maiden names* of female members are given in parentheses in the above table, in cases where they were not changed till after connection with the church.

* Deceased, August 10, 1865.

INDEX OF NAMES.

INDEX OF SUBJECTS.

www.ingramcontent.com/pod-product-compliance
Lightning Source LLC
LaVergne TN
LVHW021404110826
845150LV00007B/1773

* 9 7 8 1 4 2 5 5 1 2 7 7 4 *